Gavin Dudeney
and Nicky Hockly

how to

teach english
with technology

PEARSON
Longman

series editor:
Jeremy Harmer

Pearson Education Limited
Edinburgh Gate
Harlow
Essex
CM20 2JE
England
and Associated Companies throughout the world.

www.longman.com

Printed in Malaysia

Second impression 2007

Produced for the publishers by Stenton Associates, Saffron Walden, Essex, UK. Text design by Keith Rigley.

ISBN: 978-1-4058-4773-5

Acknowledgements
We are grateful to the following for permission to reproduce photographs:
pg 8 Alamy Images: Nicola Armstrong (t); Bob Handelman (c); Punchstock: Pixland (b); pg 14 Alamy Images: ImageState/Robert Llewellyn; pg 24 Ardea: Clem Haagner; pg 47 Getty Images: Frazer Harrison; pg 123 Corbis: Najlah Feanny.

pg 30 Google™! search engine; pg 31 Yahoo! Inc. 2007; pg 37 www.bbc.co.uk; pg 40 www.krysstal.com; pg 55ff www.xtec.es; pg 88 http://internationalexchange.blogspot.com A Class Blog Project between students at Casa Thomas Jefferson (Brasilia) and Estrella Mountain Community College (Phoenix); pg 89 Google Blog™! weblog (t); eslblogs.org part of edublogs, free blogging services for teachers and students (b); pg 92 Google Blog™! weblog; pg 93 www.bicycle-sidewalk.com; pg 94 www.wikipedia.org; pg 95 www.etwinningwiki. pbwiki.com; pg 96f pbwiki; pg 98 www.englishcaster.com; pg 100 www.podomatic.com; pg 101 aprilfoolsday. podomatic.com; pg 105 thesaurus.reference.com; pg 117 www.oup.com; pg 118 www.learn4good.com; pg 121 Jeremy Hiebert (t); pg 127 a4esl.org; pg 130 hotpot.uvic.ca; pg 132 www.halfbakedsoftware.com; pg 139 Carl Dowse; pg 145 Yahoo! Inc. 2007/IATEFL Teacher Trainers and Educators Special Interest Group; pg 150 Valentina Dodge; pg 151 www.myspace.com; pg 155 Second Life.

Every effort has been made to trace the copyright holders and we apologise in advance for any unintentional omissions. We would be pleased to insert the appropriate acknowledgement in any subsequent edition of this publication.

Author thanks
We would like to thank colleagues and friends – both 'real' and 'virtual' – for the support, insights and ideas they have brought to our working lives and to this book.

We would also like to thank Jeremy Harmer for supporting us before and during the writing process, Katy Wright at Pearson Education for her superb management of the project and Will Capel for his insightful and efficient editing. Our thanks, also, to the multimedia and audiovisual teams at Pearson Education for their creative work on the accompanying CD-ROM. And, finally, thanks to Adrian and Helen Stenton for their excellent design work on the book.

As always, a book like this is the distillation of the combined knowledge and experience not just of the authors themselves but of all the people we have met at work, at conferences, on training courses and online – we hope we have used it wisely.

This book is for colleagues past and present, and especially the Webheads online community of teachers, many of whom you will hear on the CD-ROM.

Contents

Introduction

Technology is becoming increasingly important in both our personal and professional lives, and our learners are using technology more and more. Yet teacher training programmes often ignore training in the use of Information and Communications Technology (ICT), and teachers are often far less skilled and knowledgeable than their own students when it comes to using current technology. This book bridges that gap by providing clear, non-technical descriptions of new technology tools, and by showing how teachers can use these new tools in the classroom. As such, it is about the practical application of technology to teaching languages.

How to Teach English with Technology has been written for teachers, teacher trainers, course designers and directors of studies involved in teaching English as a foreign language, although it will also be very useful for those involved in the teaching of other languages. The book is for those who have little or no experience of ICT tools or how to use them in the classroom, and also for those with more experience in the application of ICT to teaching, who will find fresh ideas for using ICT tools, as well as references to new developments in the field. Teacher trainers and directors of studies may take the contents of the book as a guide to areas to cover in implementing ICT training with their trainees or staff.

The book is organised into 12 chapters, with Task Files at the end of the book for each chapter, and covers a very broad range of technological applications, from using a word processor to looking at Second Life. The websites referred to in the book were all live at the time of going to press, but remember that websites do disappear, and links do break. We have tried to counter this by only choosing reliable websites that are likely to have a long 'shelf life', both for the book, and in the extensive Webliography, which is on the CD-ROM at the back of this book.

If you are a less confident user of technology, we would recommend that you read Chapter 1 first to get an overview of the book and to help you decide which of the subsequent chapters to focus on. The book is organised in such a way that simpler technologies and technological applications are covered first, but you may prefer to dip into the chapters which seem most relevant to your teaching or training situation.

While having access to the Internet as you read the book or look at the CD-ROM is not essential, it certainly is an advantage. The Webliography on the CD-ROM provides you with a launch pad to a huge range of content, ideas and information.

On the CD-ROM you can hear real teachers from around the world talking about their experience of using new technology in their teaching. In addition to these recordings, there are nine video tutorials on using various pieces of software. And you can go on a tour of a dictionary and see a short video of an interactive whiteboard (IWB) in action in a classroom.

Throughout the book we mention proprietorial software programs and operating systems by name, for example Microsoft Word, Skype and Blogger. We do this to provide concrete examples of tools that teachers can use in their classrooms, and not because we are specifically endorsing these products.

We are also aware that referring to PCs (personal computers) but not to Macs (Macintosh computers) will mean some slight differences for Mac users reading this book. For example, Mac users will often have Firefox or Safari as a browser and not Internet Explorer. PC users can right click the mouse to shortcut to a context sensitive menu for an object on the screen, while Mac users need to hold down the control (or apple) key and click at the same time to access this function. However, apart from Chapter 2 where we look specifically at Microsoft Word, Mac users will find that all the other tools referred to in this book can easily be used on a Mac.

If you are using content such as photos from the Internet for your worksheets, or plan to use audio or video files from the Internet with your learners, you need to ensure that copyright is respected. The Webliography contains a link to advice on Internet copyright, and it is worth knowing that you can freely use any content which is Creative Commons licensed. The Glossary on page 183 contains all the information technology terms highlighted in bold within the twelve chapters.

Finally, we would welcome feedback on this book, and to hear about any ICT projects that you implement with your learners – let us know how it went, and what you think! Contact us at www.longman.com/methodology/.

Gavin Dudeney
Nicky Hockly

1 | Technology in the classroom

- **Technology in language teaching**
- **Attitudes to technology**
- **Implementing ICT in the classroom**
- **Skills and equipment for getting started**

Technology in language teaching

Technology in language teaching is not new. Indeed, technology has been around in language teaching for decades – one might argue for centuries, if we classify the blackboard as a form of technology. Tape recorders, language laboratories and video have been in use since the 1960s and 1970s, and are still used in classrooms around the world.

Computer-based materials for language teaching, often referred to as **CALL** (Computer Assisted Language Learning), appeared in the early 1980s. Early CALL programs typically required learners to respond to stimuli on the computer screen and to carry out tasks such as filling in gapped texts, matching sentence halves and doing multiple-choice activities. Probably one of the best-known early CALL activities is that of text reconstruction, where an entire text is blanked out and the learner recreates it by typing in words. For all of these activities the computer then offers the learner feedback, ranging from simply pointing out whether the answer is correct or incorrect to providing more sophisticated feedback, such as showing why the learner is mistaken and offering remedial activities. The CALL approach is one that is still found on many published CD-ROMs for language teaching.

As access to Information and Communications Technology (**ICT**) has become more widespread, so CALL has moved beyond the use of computer programs to embrace the use of the **Internet** and web-based tools. The term **TELL** (Technology Enhanced Language Learning) appeared in the 1990s, in response to the growing possibilities offered by the Internet and communications technology.

Although the use of ICT by language teachers is still not widespread, the use of technology in the classroom is becoming increasingly important, and it will become a normal part of ELT practice in the coming years. There are many reasons for this:

- Internet access – either in private homes, or at **Internet cafés** – is becoming increasingly available to learners.

- Younger learners are growing up with technology, and it is a natural and integrated part of their lives. For these learners the use of technology is a way to bring the outside world into the classroom. And some of these younger learners will in turn become teachers themselves.

- English, as an international language, is being used in technologically mediated contexts.

- Technology, especially the Internet, presents us with new opportunities for authentic tasks and materials, as well as access to a wealth of ready-made ELT materials.

- The Internet offers excellent opportunities for collaboration and communication between learners who are geographically dispersed.

- Technology is offered with published materials such as coursebooks and resource books for teachers.

- Learners increasingly expect language schools to integrate technology into teaching.

- Technology offers new ways for practising language and assessing performance.

- Technology is becoming increasingly mobile. It can be used not only in the classroom, lecture hall, computer room or self-access centre, it can also be used at home, on the way to school and in Internet cafés.

- Using a range of ICT tools can give learners exposure to and practice in all of the four main language skills – speaking, listening, writing and reading.

The contexts in which teachers are working with technology can vary widely, and the access that teachers have to computers – the so-called **digital divide** – will affect what we can do with our classes in terms of implementing technology. A general lack of ICT training for teachers also means that we still have some way to go until the normalisation of technology in language teaching, where the use of technology in teaching becomes as natural as the use of books or pens and paper.

Attitudes to technology

Many people are afraid of new technology, and, with the increasing presence of the Internet and computers, the term **technophobe** has appeared to refer to those of us who might be wary of these new developments. More recently, the term **digital native** has been coined to refer to someone who grows up using technology, and who thus feels comfortable and confident with it – typically today's children. Their parents, on the other hand, tend to be

digital immigrants, who have come late to the world of technology, if at all. In many cases, teachers are the digital immigrants and our younger students are the digital natives.

Think about yourself. Where do you stand? How confident do you feel about using the Internet and computers? Although there is a tendency to call computer users either **technophobes** or **technogeeks** (a term for a technology enthusiast), the truth is that most of us probably fall somewhere between the two extremes.

A large part of the negative attitudes teachers have towards technology is usually the result of a lack of confidence, a lack of facilities or a lack of training, resulting in an inability to see the benefit of using technologies in the classroom. It is also often the case that teachers may not be fully in control of their work situations. A teacher may want to use more technology in their teaching, but the school may not have the facilities, or, on the other hand, a teacher may be instructed to start using technology for which they feel unprepared or untrained.

Here are a few of the more negative comments we've heard from teachers in schools we have visited or trained in:

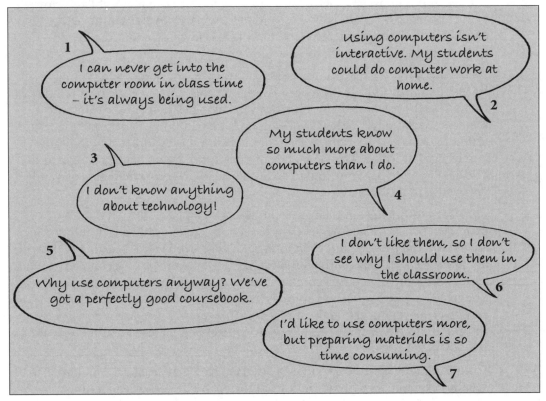

Here are our responses to these comments:

1 Timetable when you are going to use the computer room well in advance, and use a booking form which covers several months or a term. Put this booking form on the door of the **computer room** so that all teachers and learners can see when the room will be used, and by whom. You can use the computer room regularly for project work (see Chapters 4, 5 and 7), or regular self-study work (see Chapter 9).

This can easily be timetabled in advance. You might also want to negotiate with the school about the possibility of having one computer in your classroom. Some activities can be done using a single computer in the classroom.

2 Some computer-based work can be done alone, for example using **CD-ROMs** (see Chapter 9), but a lot of ideas for using technology and the Internet explored in this book involve pair- and small-group work. The ideal scenario is to have one computer available per pair of learners, but many activities can also be carried out using a single computer with a whole class, or with small groups of learners (three to four) per computer.

3 This is an often-heard remark, and reflects a very real lack of training in the classroom use of technology in ELT. When pressed, teachers usually admit that they do in fact know a bit about technology – they usually know how to use **email**, a **word processing program** and the Internet. This knowledge is certainly enough to get started with using technology in the classroom, as you will see in this book. The lack of ICT training in ELT is an issue which is slowly being addressed by training bodies, and there are also several **online** teacher development groups dedicated to exploring and learning about the use of technology in the classroom for teachers to join (see Chapter 11).

4 This remark is often true for teachers who teach younger adults, or young learners, and who, like the teacher making comment 3, may have received no training in the use of technology. However, having learners in the class who know more about technology than you do is no bad thing. When starting to use technology in the classroom, teachers can rely on these more technologically knowledgeable learners for help and support. Learners are usually delighted to be called upon to help out, and to get a chance to demonstrate their skills and knowledge in this area.

5 The use of technology in the classroom does not replace using traditional materials such as a black/whiteboard or a coursebook – rather, technology tools are used to *complement* and *enhance* regular classroom work. Imagine that a unit in the coursebook deals with animals in danger of extinction. Technology can be used to do complementary activities such as a data collection email project (see Chapter 5), or a **webquest** on animals in danger of extinction (see Chapter 4) or even to create a **podcast** on the topic (see Chapter 7). The teacher can produce additional electronic materials to review coursebook material on the topic, too (see Chapter 10).

6 This dislike and fear of computers is often expressed by teachers who have had negative experiences with technology in the past. The best way to address the situation is to make teachers aware that they already *have* certain technical skills – they probably know how to use a tape recorder in the classroom, for example, and often already use technology in their personal lives, such as an **MP3 player**, the Internet or email. In other words, rather than dismissing very real fears, these need to be acknowledged and addressed. The technophobic teacher needs to be encouraged to get started by implementing simple, undemanding technology with learners. Using a ready-made webquest from the Internet, for example, is a

good way to start (see Chapter 4). Teachers also need to realise that technology does and will break down occasionally, and that it's always good to have a backup plan that doesn't require the use of technology. Also, providing good training in the use of technology in the classroom through face-to-face workshops or online courses is key to encouraging the long-term acceptance and use of technology by technophobic teachers (see Chapter 11).

7 Making new materials from scratch can be time-consuming, both for paper-based classes and for classes using technology. Teachers need to collaborate in schools and pool resources and lesson plans, as well as use the technology-based resources that most commercial coursebooks provide nowadays. Typically, a coursebook will have its own web pages on the publisher's website, a list of recommended websites to visit for each unit, a CD-ROM and/or **DVD**, and occasionally teacher support online, in the form of frequently asked questions (FAQs), or discussion forums.

Implementing ICT in the classroom

As we know, teachers have varying levels of access to computers and technology, and teach in all sorts of contexts to all sorts of learners. Here are some of the questions you may be asking yourself about using technology in the classroom.

How can I use ICT with my class if there is only one computer in the school?

Introducing a rota or booking system for the computer with your colleagues will ensure equal use for all the teachers in the school. You will need to use the Internet mainly as a resource with your learners, accessing the Internet to download and print out materials to use offline with classes. Technology-based activities you can do by printing off materials include:

- using **websites** (see Chapter 3).
- Internet-based project work – especially webquests offline (see Chapter 4).
- email **keypal** projects using the teacher's email account (see Chapter 5).
- a class **blog** with learners preparing their contributions on paper and the teacher typing them into the computer (see Chapter 7).
- using online reference tools such as **concordancers** on paper (see Chapter 8).
- electronically produced materials printed out for learners (see Chapter 10).

You can also join free online teacher development groups (see Chapter 11).

What can I do if my learners have very low Information Technology (IT) experience and skills?

You need to first find out about your learners' IT skills and degrees of experience, for example by means of a questionnaire, and then start off by using the simplest technologies in the classroom. For learners with zero or very low IT skills, or literacy issues, a good place to start is with simple word processing tasks (see Chapter 2). Once learners are comfortable with this, basic email (see Chapter 5) or searching the Internet (see Chapter 3) can be introduced. Try to pair up more technically experienced learners with the absolute novices for any ICT-based classwork, so that the more experienced users help the less experienced ones.

I teach classes of 30+ students. How can I use computers with such large groups?

You will need to have access to a minimum number of computers, with no more than four learners per computer doing small-group work online. Large classes, with more than 30 students, can be divided into two groups – while one group is doing online computer room work, the other group is doing paper-based work. The two groups then change over. You will be able to implement most of the tools and activities described in this book.

I'm keen to use ICT in the classroom, but don't know where to start! Could you suggest what I try first?

If you don't have much experience of ICT, we would suggest starting with simple tools and projects in class, such as using websites (see Chapter 3), or using ready-made materials for language learners, such as webquests (see Chapter 4). You might also want to start using email with your learners, simply for receiving and marking work, or for simple collaborative writing projects (see Chapter 5).

I don't have much time for material preparation. What chapters in this book would you recommend I read first?

Using ICT-based activities does not mean that completely new materials need to be prepared for every class. The Internet has a wealth of ready-made materials available – you simply need to know how to find them! First hone your Internet search and evaluation skills (see Chapter 3), then look for ready-made materials to use with your classes, such as webquests (see Chapter 4) or technology-based courseware (see Chapter 9), or use simple tools that need little or no preparation, such as email (see Chapter 5) or chat (see Chapter 6).

What types of ICT tools and activities would you recommend as best for young learners?

All of the ICT tools, and many of the activities, discussed in this book are suitable for use with young learners – indeed many of today's young learners are more tech-savvy than their teachers! You might want to ask your young learners what tools they already know or use, and start off by using those. Many teenagers, for example, will already be familiar with email, **instant messaging** and **chat**, and perhaps even with blogs. For younger learners, you may want to use some of the ready-made materials and websites available on the Internet for this age group. There are also plenty of webquests on a range of topics available for younger learners.

I'd like to use the Internet to put my learners in touch with learners in other countries. How can I do this?

Several Internet tools provide an excellent way to put learners in contact with learners from other countries and cultures, as well as providing them with realistic and motivating opportunities to practise their English. The simplest way to set up a project between classes is via email (see Chapter 5) but this can be extended into collaborative projects using blogs, **wikis** or even chat (see Chapters 6 and 7). Joining an online teacher development group (see Chapter 11) will make it easy for you to contact other teachers around the world, and to set up these kinds of projects.

My learners need to use the computer room mainly for self-study or research, without a teacher being present. What can they do on their own?

There may be times when learners are scheduled to work alone on computers in a self-access centre. Typically, CD-ROMs (see Chapter 9) are provided for these occasions. In some schools students can access content placed on a central school **server** via an Intranet. However, if the computers are linked to the Internet, learners can also be encouraged to work on Internet-based projects in pairs, such as:

- webquests (see Chapter 4).
- electronic materials developed by the teacher especially for these students (see Chapter 10).
- research for later presentation to the class, using online dictionaries or other reference tools (see Chapter 8).

They could also be listening to podcasts, preparing and updating their personal blogs or developing a class wiki (see Chapter 7), or even using text chat (see Chapter 6).

Skills and equipment for getting started

What does a teacher need to know to be able to use technology in the classroom? Well, you don't need to have any specialist technical knowledge or skills, much as you don't need to be a mechanic to know how to drive a car!

The basic skills you do need to have in place before you start reading this book are how to use a simple word processing program (e.g. Microsoft Word), how to use email and how to access and use the Internet. By reading this book, and trying out the activities suggested with your learners (with plenty of step-by-step help provided in the tutorials on the CD-ROM if you feel you need it), you should be able to greatly increase your ICT skills set, and to feel a lot more confident about using technology in the classroom.

You will also need some essential equipment in order to get the most out of this book, and to start to implement technology with your learners:

- at least one computer (preferably one per two students).
- an Internet connection.
- a printer.
- an audio card in the computer, and a headset (audio and microphone) for every computer.
- basic software (a word processing program, a **web browser** like Internet Explorer, Firefox, Safari or Mozilla, and an email program).

As we saw above, teaching contexts and teachers' access to computers and technology can vary widely. While reading this book, you'll find plenty of activities which can be done if only one computer is available in class. However, access to a computer room to which you can take your class will provide more opportunities for implementing technology, for both you and your learners.

It is worth bearing in mind that the layout of your computer room will directly affect the types of activities you are able to do with your learners, and how they interact with one another and with you. A layout which has computers at desks around the walls, facing the walls, with a large table in the centre of the room, allows the teacher to walk around and easily see what the learners are working on and what they're looking at on the computer monitors (screens). The central area provides an easily accessible space where learners can go when they don't need the computers, and for when we might want to do more communicative group work. If the central space is reasonably large, more movement and activity is possible in the

centre of the room; this will offer up more opportunities for kinaesthetic learners, and the chance to use games and physical activities with younger learners away from the computer monitors.

Of course, few of us are lucky enough to be able to choose how our computer facilities look, but it may be possible for you to make some small changes in the work environment so that it's more comfortable to work in the room, and easier to teach in. It's well worth considering how your institution's computer room could be made more user-friendly for you and your classes.

Conclusions | *In this chapter we have:*

- considered the causes of technophobia and suggested ways of overcoming it.
- examined specific teacher doubts about using technology in the classroom and suggested some solutions.
- looked at a variety of EFL teaching contexts and teachers' access to computers, and discussed the types of computer-based activities you can do with your learners.
- outlined the basic skills and equipment that teachers need in order to start using technology in their teaching.

> ON THE CD-ROM YOU CAN HEAR THREE TEACHERS TALKING ABOUT THEIR USE OF TECHNOLOGY IN THE CLASSROOM.

Word processors in the classroom

- ■ **Why use word processors?**
- ■ **Word processors for teachers: creating materials**
- ■ **Word processing activities for learners**
- ■ **Using word processors: considerations**

Why use word processors?

In many ways it may seem paradoxical to devote an entire chapter to the use of word processors, when there are so many other more exciting software tools one could turn to. Yet word processors can be used in many inventive ways, by both teachers and students. Teachers can prepare, create, store and share materials for their classes by using a word processing program, and learners can use a word processing program both in and outside the classroom, to practise writing skills, grammar and other language points, as well as to present their work.

Also, most teachers and learners these days will be familiar with the basic functions of a word processing program, and know how to create, save and store documents, which makes a program like this a good starting point. In this chapter we assume basic knowledge of creating and saving documents, and focus on how to use word processing software efficiently and creatively, introducing you to word processing features you may not be aware of, but which are particularly useful for both language teachers and learners.

We will be focusing on **Microsoft Word**. Although not everyone uses Microsoft Word, it is currently the most ubiquitous of word processing packages, with an estimated 300 million users worldwide at the time of writing. However, the processes and tools we discuss in this chapter will be similar in other word processing software packages, like **OpenOffice**.

A lot of the activities we will be examining here envisage one or two learners to a computer, but with some thought they can be adapted to the single-computer classroom, or assigned as homework if your learners have access to computers at home.

Word processors for teachers: creating materials

As a teacher, you may already use a word processing program to prepare worksheets and materials for your learners. You may also use one for correcting, editing and providing feedback on your learners' digitally submitted written work. In this section, we will look at both of these two 'teacher' uses of word processors.

Inserting images and links

Two of the things you will probably want to do when creating materials are to incorporate images into your worksheets to brighten them up, and to include links to websites which your students can go to for further research or practice.

Images can be incorporated from your own computer (if you have a collection of them) or from Internet sources (copyright permitting). To insert an image which is already stored on your own computer into a document, click the 'Insert' menu, then select 'Picture' and finally 'From file …' . You will now be able to browse your computer for any pictures you may have stored on it. To grab an image from the Internet, simply find a page with the image, and right-click on it. A menu will pop up and you should choose 'Copy' from the menu, then return to your word processor and paste it into your document where you want it to be.

The trick with images is knowing how to make them interact with the text you have on your page, flowing the text around your images, rather than having it above and below, with your picture isolated in the middle. This is called **text wrapping**. To work with text wrapping you will first need to enable the picture toolbar: click on 'View' then 'Toolbars' and finally 'Picture'. Now select your picture by clicking on it once and look at the picture toolbar.

In the **screenshot** here we have highlighted the text wrapping option. With your picture selected, click on the 'Tight' option and watch how the text redistributes itself around the image. Now you will be able to drag the picture around your page and put it exactly where you want it to be. Try experimenting with the other text wrapping options, too. This screenshot shows the results of wrapping text around an image, leaving a small white border around each element of the image.

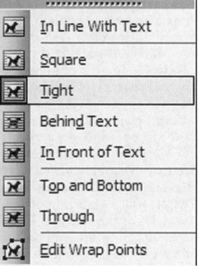

Including a web link in a document is simple and can be accomplished in a variety of ways. The easiest way of doing this is to open the website you want your learners to visit in a browser, and then click once on the address of that website in the 'Address' bar at the top of the browser. This will select the address. Now copy the address (by using Ctrl+C) and then open up your document and paste it onto the page (by using Ctrl+V). As soon as you hit the space or return key, the text you have pasted in will automatically become an active link. Note that to activate links in Word it is customary to have to hold down the Ctrl key while clicking on them.

Creating forms

A form is a Word document which has interactive elements in it, resembling closely the kinds of simple exercises you might find on the Internet. These elements can include (among others) drop-down menus for making choices, text entry fields where your learners can type in text, and buttons to select one of a set of choices.

Look at the reading exercise below, composed of a short text and a form featuring comprehension questions for learners to answer. When this is done by learners in Word, the form is locked beforehand and becomes interactive, allowing them to click on answer choices (questions 1 and 6), type answers in (questions 3 and 5) or select from a drop-down list of suggested answers (questions 2, 4 and 7). Once the form in the exercise above is 'locked', each learner can read the text and do the exercise.

Barcelona – An Introduction

Barcelona, the second largest city in Spain, is a modern and cosmopolitan place located on the north-east coast of Spain. Today almost 4.5 million people live in the Barcelona metropolitan area.

The city is 160 kilometres south of the Pyrenees mountain range, and lies at an altitude of 4 metres above sea level. The area around Barcelona has a wealth of attractions including the laid-back resort towns on the Costa Brava, north of the city towards the French border.

Barcelona is a typical Mediterranean city, not only due to its geographical location, but also because of its history and cultural influences. There are two official languages spoken in Barcelona: Catalan, generally spoken in all of Catalonia, and Castilian Spanish.

Get spectacular views over the city and the coast line from the hills of Tibidabo and Montjuich. Wander the old streets for plenty of examples of Romanesque, Gothic, Renaissance and Modernist architecture. Discover more about one of Spain's most famous architects: Antoni Gaudí.

Barcelona also has a lot of interesting museums, art galleries (with significant collections by Picasso and Miró), theatres and restaurants where you can tuck into typical Catalan and Spanish dishes. At night, enjoy some of the trendiest nightclubs and discos in Europe.

There are six beaches in Barcelona, totalling 4.2 kilometres of golden sands. They have all the facilities and services necessary for people to enjoy a pleasant and safe day at the beach.

Now answer the questions:

NAME:

1) Where in Spain is Barcelona?
   ☐ in the south-west   ☐ in the north-east   ☐ in the south-east

2) How many people live in the city?
   choose one ...

3) Which mountain range is nearest to Barcelona?
   choose one ...

4) What are the two most common languages spoken in Barcelona?
   choose one ...

5) Name a famous Barcelona architect:
   ...

6) How many beaches are there in Barcelona?
   ☐ three   ☐ four   ☐ five   ☐ six

7) How long are the beaches, in total?
   choose one ...

Now print this out and give it to your teacher, or send it by email.

NAME: Joan Andres

1) Where in Spain is Barcelona?

☐ the south-west   ☒ the north-east   ☐ the south-east

2) How many people live in the city?

2.4 million

3) Which mountain range is nearest to Barcelona?

The Pyrenees

4) What are the two most common languages spoken in Barcelona?

choose one... ⬍

| choose one... |
| Spanish and French | ous Barcelona architect:
| Catalan and French |
| English and Spanish |
| Catalan and Spanish | beaches are there in Barcelona?

☐ three   ☐ four   ☐ five   ☐ six

7) How long are the beaches, in total?

choose one...

Now print this out and give it to your teacher, or send it by email.

In this second version above the form is activated. Note that the form does not automatically check the answers. For more information on how this software tool works, see the Microsoft Office website, and the section dealing with forms (http://office.microsoft.com/en-us/assistance/HP052302701033.aspx).

To get started with adding forms to your documents, you will need to display the 'Forms' toolbar in Word. Click on 'View', then 'Toolbars' and finally 'Forms'. You will now see a new toolbar which will allow you to add various interactive choices to your page.

Forms   ▼ ✕
ab| ☑ ▤ | 🖆 | 🗹 | ▦ | 🗐 | 🄰 | ✎ | 🔒

Let's look at the more useful of these elements.

1 **Adding a text box to your form:**
    Type your question, then hit Enter and click on the 'Text Form Field' icon. You will see that it creates a small text box. Click on it, then click the 'Format' icon (fourth icon in the Forms toolbar). From here you can format what the text box does and the sort of input it expects.

2 **Adding a check box to your form:**
    Type your question, then hit Enter and click on the 'Check Box Form Field' icon.

You will see a check box appear. Type your first answer next to this. Now press the Tab key and repeat for as many answers as you need.

3 **Adding a drop-down menu to your form:**
Type your question, then hit Enter and click on the 'Drop-down Form Field' icon. Double-click the newly-created drop-down, and use the 'Drop-down item' box to add each individual choice you want to offer your learners. After you type each choice, click the 'Add' button. When you finish, click 'OK' to activate your drop-down.

These are the basic elements. When you have finished with your form, be sure to click on the 'Lock' icon to lock the form and activate it. This is the last icon on the Forms toolbar.

Forms can be very useful for making collections of basic exercises, and are a solid introduction to the more complex area of making web-based interactive materials (see Chapter 8). The advantage of creating activities using Forms is that it is simple. The disadvantage is that you cannot build in feedback to your students.

Using TrackChanges

Word comes with certain 'document tracking' or 'versioning' tools built in. These tools allow documents to be shared among a group of users, with each user's changes and edits highlighted in a different colour and identified by their initials (or by the user name used to install the word processor originally). When a document has been edited using these tools, any changes made by the second writer (format changes, word order, deletions, inserted comments, and so on) will be highlighted for the original author to see. The original author can then choose to accept or reject each suggested change.

A document featuring TrackChanges

In the screenshot on page 19 you'll see part of a document sent to a colleague, who turned on TrackChanges and made some suggestions. Notice how we can add comments to various parts of the text, delete and change sections, and format the text as well. When the document is returned, the writer can see the suggestions and decide whether they want to incorporate them or not.

You can turn these tools on in Word on a document-by-document basis by opening a document, then clicking 'Tools – TrackChanges'.

Teachers can use TrackChanges to provide feedback on a learner's written work. The learner's text can be corrected by the teacher using TrackChanges, or comments added suggesting how the learner might improve their own work. TrackChanges also offers possibilities in terms of peer review and correction of written work. A basic use of TrackChanges in Word might look like this:

- Learner A finishes her document and sends it to Learner B.
- Learner B turns on TrackChanges, edits the document and returns it.
- Learner A edits the document, accepting or rejecting Learner B's suggestions.
- Learner A sends the document to her teacher.
- The teacher turns on TrackChanges, edits the document and sends it back.
- Learner A examines her teacher's suggestions and makes a final edit.

Using Markin

This is another Windows program that aids the correction of word processed work from learners. It comes with a series of tools for marking up grammar mistakes, spelling errors, word order and other common errors, using a series of abbreviations which will be familiar to most teachers ('sp' for spelling, for example) and different colours for different types of errors. Once the teacher has finished correcting a text, it can be returned as a word processed document, or uploaded to a web server as a webpage. It can even be mailed from within the program itself.

In many ways, then, Markin can replace the TrackChanges tool we looked at above. Experimentation with both options will help you to decide which is best for you. It's worth bearing in mind that Markin was developed by teachers, and is therefore both more teacher-friendly, and more suitable for teaching purposes, than TrackChanges, which is an all-purpose tool. The advantage of TrackChanges is obviously that it is built in, and does not cost anything. Markin costs £20 at the time of writing (http://www.cict.co.uk/software/markin/index.htm).

Word processing activities for learners

As we suggested above, most learners these days will be familiar with using a word processing program for simple tasks like writing, saving and storing documents. However, before experimenting with word processors, you will need to check that your learners have some basic word processing and file management skills. It is a fact of life that many people who work with computers sometimes forget where they are saving documents, what they call them, and so on. It is particularly important when using word processors for teaching that certain systems are implemented – and skills taught – that make life easier for everybody. You may find that your students already have these skills, but it is worth checking before you start working regularly with computers. Below are a few simple word processing tips worth bearing in mind and sharing with your learners:

- Encourage your students to save their documents in a consistent way, naming them with their own name and a description of what the document contains, e.g. Joan Andres – Letter of Complaint.doc. In this way both your learners and you will be able to find their work more efficiently.

- With the price of external USB pen drives falling rapidly, it is advisable for learners to keep a copy of their work on one for themselves, so that your copy at work is the master copy, but another is stored safely off-site.

- Make sure that you check with whoever looks after your centre's computers – if you are lucky enough to have such a facility – that files are not deleted on a daily basis. Plenty of good work has been lost this way.

- Be prepared to deal with some computing terminology: *hard drive, c drive, printer, word processor, save, print*. Before each introductory class, try to identify the computer-related vocabulary that is likely to occur, and make sure that your students understand it.

Using word processors for creative writing

Word processors lend themselves well to creative writing both in and outside the classroom. As we have seen, learners can work together with documents that can be exchanged easily between pairs or groups of learners, and between learners and teachers, encouraging both teacher corrections, and peer correction and revision.

Word processors also include dictionary, grammar and thesaurus tools. Putting your cursor over the word *happy* for example, and then clicking on the 'Thesaurus' option (in Word, this is found in Tools – Language) will open up a side panel with a range of synonyms for *happy*: *content, pleased, glad, cheerful,* and so on. There is some debate on the wisdom of using these tools. The argument is sometimes made that they encourage sloppy writing and give learners too much support in the writing process itself.

A similar criticism is levelled at the spell-check option found in word processing programs. Our opinion is very much that it depends on the focus of the task and the level of the learners. Using the thesaurus option, for example, does seem to have the potential of broadening a learner's vocabulary, although the teacher may then need to address arising issues of meaning and use. In the example above, there is a difference between the meaning of *content* and *cheerful* as synonyms for *happy*. For more on electronic dictionaries and thesauruses, see Chapter 8.

If your learners are engaged in any kind of creative writing, then spell-checkers would seem to be of help in the same way that we often encourage the use of dictionaries, and professional people and other writers will use these tools as a matter of course in their day-to-day work. In these circumstances it would seem rather pointless (not to mention frustrating) to deny our learners access to these tools. Using the spell-checker on a piece of written work can make a learner more aware of errors, and provide a chance for self-correction. When using a spell-checker, learners need to ensure that they have set the language properly, for example to American or British English.

If your learners are working with word processors to practise language and structures, the spell-checker might best be turned off – at least for the first attempt at any exercise. Peer correction can be a more valuable tool in these types of activities.

It is worth pointing out these editing tools to your learners, highlighting ways of using them properly, much as we do learner training with dictionaries and other language tools, and then establishing rules for their use in your own classroom setting. One thing that we would recommend disabling is the grammar checker, which is perhaps the least reliable of these types of tool. You can do this by clicking 'Tools' then 'Options' and highlighting the 'Spelling & Grammar' tab and disabling 'Check grammar as you type'.

The basic advantage of using word processors in writing activities is the ability to model texts, share texts, produce them collaboratively and engage in peer and teacher editing on a more interactive level. Word processing activities will put the emphasis on the process of writing rather than on the final written product, for example, brainstorming, note-taking and revising, all of which makes for a more creative use of language.

Using word processors for language practice

Word processors are not only capable of enhancing writing skills, but can also be excellent tools for introducing or practising language. The ability to move words and chunks of text around the page easily can guide learners towards a deeper understanding of how the language works. The ability to undo and redo moves and edits means that experimentation is easier and less time-consuming. When used in conjunction with grammar exercises, word processors can activate 'noticing' skills, increasing awareness of language structures and encouraging learners to play with the language.

Many of the activities we do with pen and paper can work equally well on a word processor – filling in blanks, sentence reordering, adding titles to paragraphs, and so on. They also work well on another level, covering basic text manipulation skills. In this way, the use of word processors in our teaching not only serves as an aid to language practice or for the improvement of writing skills, but also teaches our learners valuable ICT skills which will carry through into other areas of their lives.

Below are two examples of activities which require text manipulation and editing in a word processing program. The first is a sample listening activity. The teacher takes

Sample listening activity	
Put the following conversation in order, then listen and check.	
JOHN: Hey! Look who's here! It's been a while!	Yeah, long time no see.
MIKE:	Working, mostly.
JOHN:	Same old stuff – you know – the book.
MIKE:	It does! How about you?
JOHN:	What have you been doing with yourself?
MIKE:	All this time? What on?
JOHN:	Not too bad. One more chapter to go.
MIKE:	How's it going?
JOHN:	Great – must feel good to be nearly done.
MIKE:	Alright for some!
JOHN:	The usual – just taking it easy …
MIKE:	

any listening dialogue from the coursebook (or another source) and types it into a word processed document. In class, learners open the document on a computer, then select and drag the sentences on the right into where they think they might go in the conversation on the left. (The first sentence of the dialogue is provided.) Learners then listen to the conversation to check.

This activity doesn't deviate significantly from the pen-and-paper model which you might find in a coursebook or in supplementary materials, but it does allow your learners to play with the text more easily, before they listen, and also covers text selection, and dragging and dropping, rather effectively. Note that this activity can be done in pairs if there are not enough computers to go around, or even in the single computer classroom with group discussion about the correct order before the text is reordered and prior to the listening phase.

Here is a sample grammar activity, in which one extra word has been added to a text. The text could be an original text, as below, or a text from the coursebook, to which the teacher adds extra words.

Sample grammar activity

Some of the lines in this text have one extra word in them. Identify and correct where necessary. The first one has been done for you.

I first ~~did~~ visited Borough Market in London on a bright spring morning in April 2004. It's an amazingly busy place, full of the people from a rich variety of countries and backgrounds – all lumped together in search of a fresh food, a new eating experience. If you're a 'foodie' then this is the most best place for you: organic ostrich steaks, olives from Spain, fresh fish, farm-made cheeses, home-made cakes and a variety of organic vegetables which all looked and smelt very fantastic. If you're not much of a cook, there are also plenty of stalls selling takeaway food from burgers to soups, sandwiches to tapas – and a lot more. If you've not never been to a modern food market, Borough is a great place for to start – the only worry is how much money you'll end up with spending, and how much weight you may put on!

Building up a collection of worksheets and activities like the ones above will allow you to give further practice, extra homework or examination preparation materials to your learners. The advantage that these materials have over many of the other options we will be looking at in the course of this book is that they are generally very small files – and so are easily transportable – and they are also more likely to fit into a wider range of computer access situations since they do not necessitate an Internet connection or high-powered computers to work.

Further activities

Dictation

A simple word processing activity to start with is a dictation from the teacher – in this case the opening few lines of a creative writing narrative. This should be treated as a standard dictation, and the learners should input (type) the text as they listen. Once you have dictated the first few lines, try introducing a small round of peer correction, with learners exchanging texts and making edits to their partner's text, possibly using TrackChanges, before moving on to a final round of teacher-led correction.

Once the dictation phase has been completed, learners return to their own documents and have a fixed period of time in which to add to your model narrative opening and to develop the story further, before turning it over once again to their partner. Their partner then has to read what has been added, make edits and is then given more time to add to the text. This process continues until completion, at which point the final product is turned in to the teacher for correction.

There is a lot of activity in this kind of process, from dictation and text modelling, through peer correction, reading, use of narrative structures and sequencing to final text production, and the combination of these techniques and skills can have a significant effect on the quality of your learners' writing.

Noticing activity

An activity which encourages noticing of structures at lower levels, and for younger learners, is for pairs of learners to produce a short descriptive text (for example of a mystery animal), including the third person -*s*.

> This animal is large and grey. It lives in Africa and India, and it has large ears and a short tail. It eats leaves and grass, and it likes to wash in the river. It remembers everything!

Pairs exchange texts, read the description and guess which animal is being described. They then underline and/or highlight all the examples of the third person -*s* they can find, either by using WordArt (in Microsoft Word), or highlighting the -*s* in a different colour, font or size. They can also be asked to search the Internet to add a photo to the highlighted text. These finished, highlighted and illustrated texts are then displayed around the classroom.

> An Elephant!
> This animal is large and grey. It live**S** in Africa and India, and it ha**S** large ears and a short tail. It eat**S** leaves and grass, and it like**S** to wash in the river. It remember**S** everything!

Collaborative writing activity

A well-known writing activity is that of the collaborative story, where a story is started (perhaps from a prompt such as an evocative series of sounds, or a painting) by one learner or pair, and then passed to subsequent pairs of learners, who add to the story. This works particularly well if learners are first asked to listen to an evocative piece of music for two or three minutes, and asked to close their eyes while they imagine what is happening, as if they were watching a film. In the computer room, after listening to the music and imagining what is happening in the film, pairs can start a story on one computer and then move around to the next computer terminal after a certain period of time (say five minutes) to add to the story on the next computer. The teacher can provide a narrative structure for each stage in front of the computer – for example:

1 Describe the scene and the characters.

[change computers]

2 What happens first in the story?

[change computers]

3 What happens as a result of this?

[change computers]

4 What new character arrives and what do they do?

[change computers]

5 How does the story end?

[change computers – go back to the story you started]

The final version of the story is then read by the pair who started it, for revision and correction, using TrackChanges, or in a copied document which is edited directly. The final edited versions of the stories are then printed out and displayed for learners to read. Learners can then compare how many different stories for the imagined film there were.

Using word processors for presenting work

One final use of word processors to consider is that of encouraging learners to put their word processed documents into a presentation package, possibly as part of an **ePortfolio** of their work. (See Chapter 9 for more on electronic portfolios.)

As we have seen, word processors facilitate correction and redrafting, and ease the pressure to produce 'good copy' in the finalised piece. They also encourage learners to take more pride in their written work, often with surprising results for those teachers used to encountering motivational difficulties when trying to get students to write.

Enhancing produced documents with images and photographs from the Internet (taking into account copyright issues) can also help to increase the time and effort put into the writing process by learners.

Specific pieces of work can easily be transferred from word processed format to a presentation format like Microsoft PowerPoint for public presentations, or added as files to students' web pages or blogs (see Chapter 7).

Once learners have a final piece of finished work as a word processed document, they can be encouraged to keep documents together in files on a USB pen drive or diskette (as well as on their own computer if they have one) as a portfolio of work produced during a course. This can then form part of their electronic portfolio, a format that is becoming increasingly important for learners in a mobile working and learning environment.

Using word processors: considerations

There are some potential downsides to using word processors – not the least of which is working with **mixed technological ability** classes where typing skills (or lack of them) may play a large part in performance anxiety and in the pace at which activities are carried out. Some attention must be paid to not putting too much pressure on your learners to perform too quickly.

You should also not expect great success with these cycles of revision and peer correction if your learners are not used to doing such activities away from the computers. In short, trying to introduce too much too quickly into your word processing classes may ultimately make them more challenging than they should be, and frustrating for your learners.

Starting with simple activities, such as the ones we looked at in the first section of this chapter, and getting your learners used to the mechanics of word processing before moving on to the more creative side, will help with this process, as will a good grounding in the writing process in the more traditional fashion.

More ideas for exploiting word processors in the classroom can be found at the following addresses:

- http://edvista.com/claire/wp.html
- http://www.geocities.com/vance_stevens/wordproc.htm

Conclusions | *In this chapter we have:*

- considered why we should use word processors in our teaching.
- looked at how teachers can work with word processors for materials creation.
- examined specific word processing tools such as inserting images and links, creating forms and using TrackChanges.
- looked at how learners can work with word processors, for creative writing, language work and presentation of work.
- considered some sample word processing activities.

> ON THE CD-ROM YOU CAN HEAR A TEACHER TALKING ABOUT USING WORD PROCESSING WITH HER LEARNERS AND WATCH A TWO-PART TUTORIAL ON TrackChanges IN Microsoft Word.

Using websites

- **Using websites in the classroom**
- **ELT websites or authentic websites?**
- **How to find useful websites**
- **How to evaluate websites**

- **Planning lessons using the Internet**
- **Working with lower levels of language proficiency**
- **Web teaching dos and don'ts**

Using websites in the classroom

In this chapter we look at the basic skillset needed for effective use of the Internet with your students and take a closer look at the process for introducing the Internet into your teaching.

Using **websites** is one of the easiest and least stressful ways of getting started with technology in the classroom. There is a large and constantly expanding collection of resources on the web, at a variety of levels and covering an amazing array of topics. You can choose from authentic (written for **Internet surfers** in general) sources or ELT-specific sites (made by, and for, teachers), monolingual or multilingual sites, sites with multimedia, or just simple text, for those on slower connections.

The **web** is a source of content which can be used as a window on the wider world outside your class, and is – of course – a readily available collection of authentic material. As such, it is a much larger repository of content than would previously have been readily available to you and your students.

Perhaps one of the best tips we can give you at this point is to work as a team with other teachers in your centre. Everybody has their favourite websites, and plenty of teachers will, at some point, have used websites in class, or taken material from the web and adapted it for teaching purposes. Take the time to share sources of content with other teachers and organise regular get-togethers where you sit down and discuss what you have found on the Internet and how you have used it in class. Collaboration like this can help to reduce the time you spend searching for good materials and the time spent preparing activities or making worksheets. Just as the Internet is becoming more of a collaborative medium, so should your use of it in your teaching.

The technology needed to use the Internet for teaching is relatively limited and the chances of something going wrong are greatly reduced over more complex technology approaches such as attempting to carry out live chat or video-conferencing sessions.

Another advantage of this tool is that you don't necessarily have to rely on a constant Internet connection if you bear in mind that it is possible to save local copies of websites on your computer, or print out potentially useful pages for later use. Indeed, you can use web pages in the classroom in a variety of ways:

- **as printed pages, with no computers**. Although printing is not necessarily the cheapest option, it is certainly a viable one in places where there may be limited access to the Internet. Indeed, a lot of activities using web pages will only necessitate the printing of one or two pages, which can subsequently be photocopied.

- **with one computer with an Internet connection**. This can be enhanced by connecting the computer to a data projector or even an interactive whiteboard, allowing for greater visibility in class, but it is also possible to make use of a single computer on its own connected to the Internet for reference.

- **in a computer lab with a set of networked and connected computers**. If you're lucky enough to be in this kind of situation, then you are ideally placed to incorporate Internet content into your regular teaching.

It's important that both you and your learners see the use of the Internet as an intrinsic part of the learning process, rather than as an occasional activity which has nothing to do with their regular study programme. We would therefore recommend that, if you plan to use the Internet, you should talk to your learners and explore the reasons for using this resource with them. This can be done at lower levels in their own language or in English with higher-level classes. You will need to talk to your learners about why Internet content may be useful to them and discuss their attitudes to technology in general – when they use computers, and what for. Show them how the coursebook and other materials can be enhanced by extra material from the Internet, but above all, make it clear that this is not a toy, not something that you are just using to fill in the time.

With some learners there may be some resistance to regular computer use in the classroom. We have often found, for example, that professional people view computers as work tools rather than as resources for learning. It is vital that they appreciate that this is a useful, as well as an entertaining, tool in the classroom and that it can contribute to their language development in a variety of ways, for example by giving them the opportunity to build vocabulary or improve their listening skills. Lower-level classes can be engaged with visual and multimedia materials, the use of songs and other video materials.

ELT websites or authentic websites?

Your choice of website will depend largely on what you want to achieve with it. Many teachers tend to steer clear of authentic websites, and by this we mean any site not created with the language learner in mind, believing that their students will find them too difficult. But, as with all authentic materials, the level and language challenges posed by these sites can be largely mitigated by the type of task you expect your learners to carry out.

A well-designed task will allow your learners to deal with authentic sites, guiding them through not only the text, but also the layout and navigation problems that may otherwise impact on their learning experience.

It is also the case that many learners these days are far more used to working with computer-based text and information than they are to dealing with more traditional, paper-based forms of text, and this familiarity with the conventions of web design can count in your favour when deciding to use authentic content from the Internet.

Of course there are plenty of ELT websites which provide content that your learners can use, for example language practice activities they can do on their own. They provide valuable opportunities for more controlled language work and are often a great help to learners who need to brush up on certain aspects of the language or to prepare for an exam. Such sites are often ideal for homework, access to the Internet permitting.

Authentic sites, on the other hand, can be chosen to fit your learners' interests. This is a key factor in keeping motivation high in your electronic classroom. When evaluating authentic sites for possible incorporation into your teaching, try to find ones which have an easy structure and navigation, and with smaller chunks of text per page. These will be more approachable and understandable. Design your tasks to make them achievable, and show your learners how they can use online dictionary sites to help them – if they need them.

Authentic sites also provide an ideal opportunity to work through the issues of 'total comprehension' that plenty of learners have to deal with at some point in their studies. They can be guided towards being comfortable with understanding the content of a site and identifying what they need to know or find out without getting bogged down in having to understand every word on the screen.

How to find useful websites

As already mentioned, the Internet is a vast repository of information and resources, and it is perhaps exactly this range that makes it seem, at first, daunting and unapproachable to most teachers. In the following two sections we take a look at how to find and evaluate resources for use in class.

The ability to search through Internet content, and quickly and efficiently find suitable resources is perhaps the most underrated, and yet most useful, skill that both teachers and learners can acquire.

For teachers, having good search skills means finding useful resources quickly, speeding up lesson planning and facilitating web use in class. For learners, it means being able to quickly accomplish web-based tasks, thus ensuring that the technology enhances the learning experience rather than impeding it. It makes sense, then, both to acquire these skills, and to spend some time sharing them with your learners.

There are three basic ways of searching on the Internet, and we will briefly describe them below, and look at ways of making searches more targeted and efficient.

Search engines

Although there is a large variety of **search engines**, perhaps the most well-known is Google (www.google.com), which currently indexes over twelve billion web pages.

A search engine is almost directly analogous to a telephone directory, or any other database of stored information. You search for a name or a title, and the directory gives you more information about that entry. But with over twelve billion pages to choose from, it's not quite as easy to use as a phone directory. So how do you find exactly what you want?

The answer comes in knowing what kind of information Google actually has on each web page that it indexes. What Google knows about a page is generally the page address on the web, the page title, when it was last updated and a few keywords associated with the content itself. These keywords are defined by the designer of the page, and can reasonably be expected to accurately reflect the content of the page. The key to good searching in Google is to define your keywords properly.

Say you have a class project on the history of the Olympic Games and you want to focus on the Barcelona games which took place in 1992. This means that instead of searching for *olympic games*, you should try something more specific: *Barcelona olympic games 1992*. In this example, more is less: the more keywords you put into the search box, the fewer page results you will get. *Olympic games* gives 30,500,000 pages, whereas *Barcelona olympic games 1992* gives 619,000 and *Barcelona olympic games 1992 10000 meters women's gold medal winner* gives 738 – with the name of the winner (Derartu Tulu – result two) clearly visible in the top few results.

The other technique which you may find useful is to use the 'phrase' search technique which involves wrapping part of a phrase in inverted commas, thus ensuring that Google will treat the words not as individual entities, but will actually look for sentences on web pages which contain those words in that particular order.

Thus, instead of searching for *cheap hotel in Rome*, which can search for any or all of these words, in any position and order, on a page, try searching for "cheap hotel in Rome" as part of a phrase you might expect to find on a web page.

To elaborate on our example above, "Barcelona olympics marathon" returns only twelve pages, since the likelihood of these three words being on a web page in this exact order is significantly smaller than the chance of the words being on a page separately in any position.

This technique is particularly useful for finding song lyrics, where searching for "I never meant to cause you trouble" will return 11,800 results, with the first result being the lyrics of the Coldplay song, whereas a search for *Coldplay lyrics* will give you access to 7,640,000 websites, but you will have to visit each one to see if that particular song lyric is there.

The ultimate trick with Google is to try to imagine the web page you are looking for, and then try to visualise the content that is on this ideal page. This technique will help you decide on exactly what to search for.

In our next example, one learner is doing a project on the singer, Shakira, and needs some biographical information. Searching for Shakira on Google returns 43,200,000 pages. But how exactly would biographical information be presented on a website? Perhaps a search for "Shakira was born in" would be more useful, since the only possible information which could follow such a phrase would be a location or a date. This search returns 266 results, with the first few all leading to biographies of the singer.

Subject guides

Yahoo! (www.yahoo.com) currently claims to index nearly twenty billion pages, and is still the search venue of choice for many people who remember when it was the only way of searching the Internet. The approach here is slightly different in that Yahoo! was never intended as a keyword search engine, but rather as a way of browsing titles. Whereas Google might be likened to a telephone directory, a more familiar metaphor for Yahoo! would be that of the library, where users have a notion of what they are looking for, but not necessarily the exact title. So, in that sense, we are invited to browse, to wander around, rather than directly key in search terms or words we are interested in exploring.

Yahoo! derives its description of **subject guide** from the fact that it divides its content into subject areas, and subdivisions of those areas. Instead of a keyword search from the main page, users browse the section which best reflects their interests, and then search.

Using Yahoo! to find our biographical information about Shakira, we would access the Yahoo! directory by clicking on the *more* dropdown list at the top of the Yahoo! main page and choose *Directory*. From there we can browse to Shakira: click on *Entertainment*, then *Music* then *Artists*, and finally search for Shakira biography, making sure to select the *this category* option. What this essentially means is that Yahoo! will only search in 'Entertainment – Music – Artists' rather than in its entire directory. This yields six results, shown below, all of which lead to biographies of the singer.

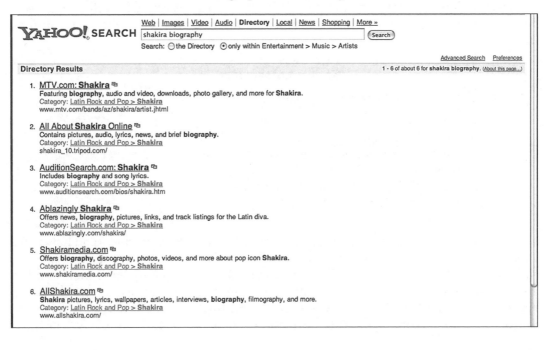

It is worth noting that Yahoo! search results can often be more accurate than Google results as they tend to lead searchers to the first page of a website, rather than dropping them indiscriminately into the middle, where the chances of confusion are higher.

Real language searches

A real language search such as **Ask** (www.ask.com) allows the user to type simple questions as search queries. Thus our learner who is investigating the life and times of Shakira types something along the lines of *When was Shakira born?* instead of a selection of appropriate keywords. Note that the website does not actually analyse or indeed understand the question itself, but rather selects the keywords from the query ('when', 'Shakira', 'born') and constructs a search based on them.

A search on Ask should give you a results page with the answer to your question at the top (where Ask has been able to find a direct answer), and links to relevant sites below that.

Your choice of search facility will depend on how you like to work, and which site you find particularly attractive and useful. However, it is worth taking the time to play with all three and to spend some time exploring them with your learners. Learners can benefit from an exposure to all three types, as they activate different linguistic and mental processes. Keywords are good for exploring word relationships and lexical areas. Subject searches help define and refine ideas and contexts. A real search can provide useful practice in question formation.

A simple way of introducing the topic of searching the Internet in class is to produce a trivia quiz or short 'treasure hunt' type activity for your learners to do. Give them a set of questions and allow them to use all three search pages to find the answers. Make it into a timed quiz, with the first team to finish bringing the activity to an end. Then go over the answers and help them to see how to improve their search skills.

It is at this point that you can examine which search page was used in each case, if it was the appropriate choice, and work together as a group to extrapolate general conclusions about search techniques.

Sample treasure hunt

Use your search skills to find this information:

- the name of the president of the World Bank.
- the capital of Scotland.
- the country that won the 1986 FIFA World Cup.
- the author of *Of Mice and Men*.
- nationality of the architect of 'La Pedrera'.
- the director of the movie *North by Northwest*.

In this example we can see how a variety of approaches would be possible – and how these might lead to a useful discussion on search skills, as well as some basic language work, on question formation, for example. The first search encourages the use of Google and the 'part of a sentence' approach discussed above, with perhaps the best search term being "*is the president of the World Bank*", while the second one might work nicely as a real language search, with learners coming up with the question *What's the capital of Scotland?* The third search involves reformulation to be successful, perhaps *Who won the 1986 FIFA World Cup?* These are the skills which are the basis of many of the activities you will do on the Internet, so it is worth spending some time refining them and examining them a little more closely.

It is also worth considering specialist sites as a source of information. Teach yourself and your learners to think a little more laterally. For example, any queries related to movies might be better directed to the Internet Movie Database (www.imdb.com) than a search engine. Similarly, book information can be easily found on the Amazon site (www.amazon.com), and football World Cup information on the FIFA site (www.fifa.com).

Variations on this treasure hunt activity include learners then making a quiz for another team to do. They must be able to find the answers themselves before they hand over the task to the other team. Or the whole class could make a quiz for you, the teacher, to do as homework! This can be a highly motivating task for learners, as they pit themselves and their Internet skills against the teacher's.

There are also subject- or media-specific search sites which are worth having a quick look at, though do bear in mind that much of what you find on media search sites will be subject to copyright, so please check the terms of use before including anything in any materials you might make. You might like to try the following to get started:

- http://images.google.com/ – Google image search, allows you to search an enormous collection of images in various formats. A good place to start looking for illustrations for worksheets, teaching materials, projects or presentations.

- http://froogle.google.com/ – Google shopping search, gives you access to comparative shopping results for products. Use this to find products you are interested in, read reviews and find the best prices.

- http://video.search.yahoo.com/ – Yahoo! video search allows you to search a large database of online video material by keyword or category. Ideal if you want to demonstrate something in a more lively way, for music videos and other multimedia classes.

- http://www.altavista.com/video – AltaVista video search works in the same way as the Yahoo! one above, but videos are also classified by different formats, allowing for a range of multimedia players and software to be used to watch them.

- http://www.altavista.com/audio/default – AltaVista audio search gives you access to a large online collection of audio files. Particularly good for searching for the popular MP3 format song files.

- http://search.singingfish.com/sfw/home.jsp – Singing Fish multimedia search, combining both audio and video results in one interface. It has a large collection of sources, and you can search by category, including movies, news, TV, sports and a host of others.

- http://tv.blinkx.com/ – Blinkx TV video search allows you to search popular TV broadcasters like the BBC and CNN for short video clips on a wide variety of subjects. Again, this is an ideal source of news material.

You may also like to try one of the **meta search** sites. These are sites which search more than one search engine at the same time, giving you, for example, the ability to search Yahoo!, Google and Ask from one single page. Examples include:

- http://www.dogpile.com/ – Dogpile.
- http://www.kartoo.com/ – KartOO.
- http://www.mamma.com/ – Mamma.

You will, of course, get far more results than if you simply used one single search engine, but you will also get a sense of balance from a meta search engine, as the results come from a variety of sources using a variety of search techniques. You will tend to get a more rounded view of what is out there on the Internet. Concentrating on the first couple of pages of results will help reduce the potentially overwhelming quantity of data returned.

One final hint: whenever you visit a search engine, be sure to click on the help link to see what hints and tips the site owners recommend for improving your search techniques.

How to evaluate websites

Having found potentially useful websites, the next step is to evaluate how useful and appropriate they are for the classroom. You will also need to think about the aims and objectives of your lesson. Does the website you have found fit in with these, and does it enhance and complement the other materials and activities you have planned for the class? Sometimes the Internet content will be the core of a particular lesson but at other times it will merely serve as a jumping-off point into something more closely related to a particular coursebook theme or unit, or be a source of extra material to follow up on the core classroom content. There are various standard criteria for judging websites which can serve as a starting point for your evaluation:

1 Accuracy

- Who wrote the page? Is this person an expert in the subject matter?
  Check qualifications, experience – look for an 'about me' link.

- Is the page content reliable and factually correct?
  Cross-reference with other similar websites and encyclopedias.

2 Currency

- Is the content up-to-date?
  Check factual information against other reliable sources.

- When was the page last updated?
  Check for information at the bottom/top of the page.

3 Content

- Is the site interesting and stimulating?
  Consider the content from your learners' point of view.

- Is it attractive and easy to navigate?
  Check the colour combinations, the logic of the links and visual structure.

4 Functionality

- Does the site work well? Are there any broken links?
  Be sure to check all pages, and follow all links to all pages you intend to use.

- Does it use a lot of large files or alternative technologies (e.g. Flash)?
  Check how quickly it loads for learners; check sound, video and animation work.

It may well be that the accuracy and currency criteria, both essentially factual, are not of interest to you if you are working on a purely linguistic level, that is planning a class that exploits the language of the site, rather than the content itself. On the other hand, accuracy and currency might be the most important criteria if learners are taking notes and interpreting information in preparation for producing a project.

Another thing to bear in mind as a language teacher will be the linguistic accuracy of the web page. If this is important to you, you will need to add this to your evaluation criteria. This again will depend on the purpose of the site in your lesson plan. This is an area of contention among teachers, and a subject that almost always crops up in technology training sessions. Only you can really decide on the linguistic content of a particular site. Spending lots of time on a site devoted to mobile phone texting language with a class preparing to do an examination is probably not in the best interests of the learners, for example.

As far as content is concerned, note that criteria such as ease-of-use and interest are taken into account, but you may also want to consider adding a further set of criteria here along the lines of appropriateness. In this subcategory you would note which groups or levels the site would be suitable for and any problems you foresee with the site itself.

Functionality will be a category with consequences for all teachers. Not only can it be very frustrating to follow through the content of a site to be met with broken links and missing information, but it can be equally frustrating to wait twenty minutes for a short video to download due to the speed of your connection. Again, careful preparation and investigation in the lesson planning stage can go a long way towards making the learners' experience enjoyable and trouble-free.

However you evaluate the usefulness of the websites you find, make sure that you keep a record of the content and address so that you begin to build up a large stock of evaluated sites.

Planning lessons using the Internet

By this stage you will have found, evaluated and decided on a collection of web pages which you want to use as part of your teaching. The next area to consider is how a technology-based lesson plan will look in comparison with the sort of plans you usually produce. What will the differences be? What might go wrong, and how will you deal with it?

The first thing, of course, is to plan your session well: visit the websites you intend to use and make sure you know your way around them properly. Try to use sites which appear to have a potentially long 'shelf life' – ones made by large institutions and commercial organisations, rather than personal homepages, which have a tendency to come and go with alarming frequency.

Make a note of the particular pages you want your learners to work on – you can use the Favorites option in Internet Explorer, or Bookmarks in Firefox to log web addresses for later use – and make sure you're familiar with the content. Your ability to answer questions as they arise will add to your confidence and also inspire confidence in your learners.

Planning a web-based lesson, rather than one where the web content plays an ancillary role, is not intrinsically different from planning a more traditional one. We like to divide a typical web-based session into three parts (www): warmer, web, what next.

The warmer part of the lesson is the kind of thing we all do as a matter of course, with introductory activities, interest-generating ideas, and so on. This part prepares your learners for what they are going to be doing in the web part of the lesson. Our view is that this part of the lesson is best done in the familiar environment of the normal classroom.

In the web section of the lesson, it's important to spend only as much time as you need working with the computers. We prefer to take learners to a computer room for this part rather than spend the entire class in there. This has the double advantage of allowing more groups to use the room and of keeping learners focused during their time there. It is also an opportunity for learners to stretch their legs and provides a change of pace. On the other hand, moving from the traditional classroom to a computer room does have the potential to disrupt your class, so careful planning of the logistics may be necessary.

If you have limited access to computers, or perhaps only one computer in the classroom, you can print off the web-based materials you want to use with your learners in advance, and simply use a print version. This is, of course, not as exciting as using computers themselves, but can bring the Internet into more resource-poor environments.

Of course, there are certain teaching situations where teachers are obliged to take their learners to a computer facility for one or more lessons per week. If you do find yourself in this position, you can adapt your lesson plans to make greater use of the Internet than we are suggesting here.

You may even choose to incorporate the use of websites more consistently into the curriculum of the course you are teaching – perhaps substituting a part of the course materials you are using for websites, for example the reading texts or the listening material. However you decide to do this, it must be a transparent process for the learners, and they must be able to appreciate not only the thought processes that have gone into this decision, but also the relevance and value of the change. This can be achieved in part by helping learners to cast a critical eye over the materials they work with in class, and encouraging them to talk about what they like doing and what they don't.

It should also be born in mind that your learners will have favourite websites of their own, and it is well worth investigating whether these can be incorporated into your classroom teaching, partly as a motivator, but also as a link to their lives, interests and experiences outside the class. This again will help them to see the value of the technology applied in class.

It's worth remembering that once you put people behind computer monitors, it's easy for them to forget that you are there, and – more importantly – why they are there. So the two vital words here are time and task. Make sure your learners have a clearly-defined task to achieve and a clearly-defined time frame in which to achieve it.

Once the group has got what you intended from the computers, it's time to move them back to the classroom for the what next stage of the lesson. This part should deal with the tasks set for the web part and then proceed with more familiar follow-up activities to round off the lesson.

Movie stars is a sample lesson plan based on this structure. You can use this as a template for your own planning. It is worth noting that there is nothing intrinsically different from the more traditional coursebook approach here – perhaps the major value of this material is its intrinsic motivational element: real actors being interviewed for a real programme. This, plus the contemporary nature of most website content, make the web an ideal source of material.

A lesson plan – Movie stars

This is an upper-intermediate to advanced lesson concentrating on famous movie stars and their lives and work. The language areas covered are: asking and answering questions, reacting to information, and showing interest. Learners will also explore interview techniques, and ways of interacting on a social level. The class uses the BBC website, and its section devoted to The Film Programme on BBC Radio 4, which you can see below.

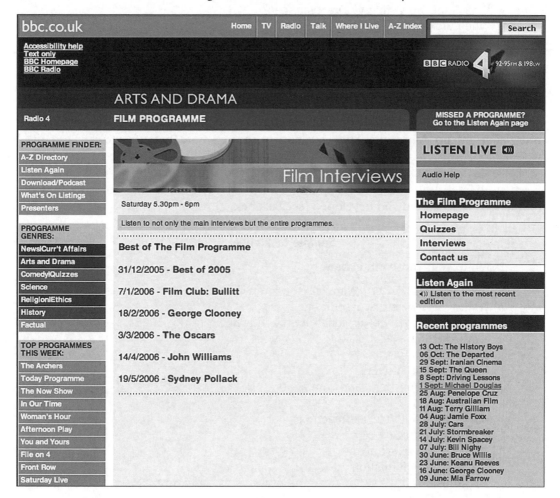

Warmer

Introduce the subject by talking about learners' favourite movie stars and their work. At this level, a simple class discussion will work fine, but be prepared to prompt with various subject areas: favourite movies, recent visits to the cinema, forthcoming films, best and worst films, and so on.

Sample warmer

Talk to your partner.

- What kind of films do you like?
- Who are your favourite actors?
- What's the best film you've ever seen?
- What's the worst film you've ever seen?
- When did you last go to the cinema?

Which movie star would they like to interview, given the chance, and what would they ask that person?

Web

Have your learners visit the site and find an actor they are interested in – these are all audio interviews, with no transcripts. There is plenty of choice – note that interviews are archived by year.

Let each learner choose an interview to listen to, and ask them to make notes on the main themes dealt with, and to examine how the interview is constructed – how the interactions were started and developed (see task below).

Sample task sheet

Listen to your chosen interview.

- Who was interviewed? Who was the interviewer?
- What topics were discussed?
- How did the interviewer construct the interview?
  - introduction
  - initial questions
  - reactions to answers
  - follow-up questions and comments
  - conclusions
- How did the interviewee react?
  - getting started
  - answers to questions
  - additional information
  - conclusions
- Make a note of some of the useful interview expressions.

What next

Give each learner a chance to report back on what they listened to, who was interviewed and what the main themes of the interview were. What did they find out and what would they have liked to have found out, but didn't?

Developing a conversation with someone is a difficult skill to acquire in another language. Elicit some of the ways they heard the interviewer and interviewee working together to construct the dialogue. Write some of the language and techniques up on the board and analyse structures, purpose, and so on.

There are plenty of follow-up activities to do here, including:

- speaking activity: an interview.
  Give each pair a role (famous person or interviewer) and have them conduct an interview. This could also be recorded or videoed for later language work.

- writing activity: 'a day in the life'.
  This is often seen in UK Sunday newspaper supplements, where a famous person is interviewed about a day in their life, or a particularly interesting day in the past week.

- writing activity: an interview.
  As for the speaking activity above, but styled for a magazine or newspaper. This could be done individually, or in pairs – with one writing the questions, the other the answers. This could be presented as an email interview.

- writing activity: a biography.
  A more formal written piece, exploring the life of a famous person. This might involve more research on the Internet.

Working with professionals at higher levels, you might also like to consider the differences in language and register between a social interview like the one they listened to and a more formal job interview.

Working with lower levels of language proficiency

One of the most often asked questions is if it is possible to work with lower-level classes and the Internet. The simple answer is that it is, of course, feasible but that the choice of websites will be far more limited than for higher levels.

A familiar worry for lower levels is how much of a given text the students will understand. Lower-level learners often feel they have to understand everything and this will lead to problems, if not dealt with beforehand.

Choosing the right websites can go some way towards raising their comfort levels, though you may need to have shorter lessons than the higher level one described above. Websites which are more suitable for lower levels will include:

- websites with simple, clearly presented text.

- websites with non-linguistic data which is easy to interpret (e.g. data in the form of a chart, such as a weather page).

- websites with visuals – a task can be based around the visuals only.

- ELT websites, where the content has been written, edited and prepared with this audience in mind.

Borrowed words

This is a low-level lesson concentrating on different languages and the words they have contributed to English. The language areas covered are countries and languages. The class uses the KryssTal: Borrowed Words in English website:

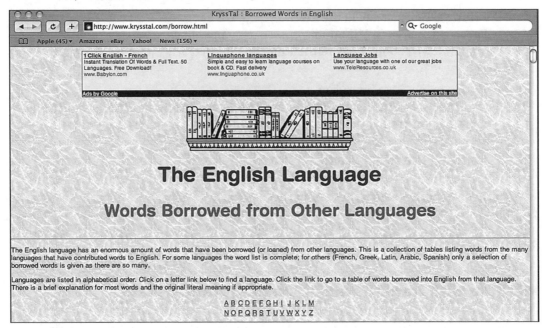

Warmer

Ask your learners if they know of any words in their own language that have come from other languages. Build up a chart on the board. You may need to help with the English versions.

Original country	Original language	Original word	Your country	Your language	Word in your language	English version
Spain	Spanish	paella	Sweden	Swedish	paella [spansk maträtt]	paella

Web

Put the learners into pairs (Student A and Student B) and give each learner a copy of the chart opposite. Give them time on the website to complete their column, leaving the other column blank for the next phase of the activity. Note that they will not only need to identify the language and country for the given words, but also find words to go with the given languages or countries.

Borrowed words in English

Use the website to complete your part of the table.

Student A				Student B		
Word	Country	Language		Word	Country	Language
kidnap				sauna		
		Greek			Japan	
lottery						Russian
	Italy			parachute		
paper					Norway	

In the next phase they will need to ask their partner questions to complete the other half of the chart. Go over the questions they will need to ask, as in the examples (for Student A) given below:

- What language does the word *sauna* come from?
- What country does *parachute* come from?
- Can you tell me a Russian word used in English?

Give each pair some time to ask and answer the questions, and complete the table. Provide feedback on a model table on the board and help out with any vocabulary problems which may have arisen.

What next

This is an ideal opportunity to do more work with the country and language vocabulary areas covered above. You may also want to brainstorm English words which are currently used in your learners' languages, and build up their collective vocabulary in this way.

An additional follow-up project idea is for learners to 'collect' English words they find in their environment, if they live in a non-English speaking country, e.g. English words on TV, or on advertising billboards and signs. These could be added to a poster in the classroom.

Web teaching dos and don'ts

Planning carefully and adopting a structured approach to the way you use websites in the classroom should give you the confidence to try out different ways of introducing your learners to Internet content.

Most of the time you will be using websites to provide your learners with knowledge and content which they perhaps do not know, or would normally not have access to, or to supplement more traditional course materials. This can be highly motivating for them, leading to more language production and a higher stake in the success of the class.

It is worth bearing in mind that it is not necessarily the 'all-singing, all-dancing' websites – ones with a lot of animation, video, audio or other multimedia content – which will be of most interest or use in your classrooms. Don't discount simple text-based websites which might be very beneficial in your own context. Apart from anything else, they are less likely to malfunction or cause problems when you go to use them.

However, having said all this, things can and sometimes do go wrong. To round off this chapter, here are a few considerations and some contingency plans:

1 Whenever you use technology you should always have a backup plan in place. There might be times when the websites are down, or the computers crash or, worse still, the electricity goes off. So be prepared.

2 Use the knowledge of other teachers and of your learners to help you with the technical side of the lesson. We often team teach with less experienced teachers, taking care of the small technical problems which occasionally arise, and leaving them free to enjoy the technology and to teach. Asking tech-savvy learners to assist takes the pressure off you and also gives them some investment in the successful outcome of the class.

3 If it's a lesson that involves relatively few web pages, try saving them to your computer hard disk. From Internet Explorer, choose 'File…' 'Save As…' then give the file a name and make sure the 'Web Page, complete' option is selected. This will save the web page and all its images and you'll be able to open the pages even if the connection goes down. You could even go so far as to print them out.

4 Unless you are working on something like an email pen pal exchange, it is rarely conducive to have learners working alone on computers. Pairs are best, but three to a computer can also work fine – just make sure that everyone gets a turn in the 'driving seat'. Pairwork and small-group work will help to encourage oral communication and break down the 'computer as barrier' effect often prevalent in technology-based classes. For the one computer classroom, use of the computer can be rotated between small groups, with the groups who are not working on the computer occupied with other stages of the same lesson, for example preparing a poster or text.

5 As was mentioned in Chapter 1, try to arrange the computer room in such a way that you can easily maintain control over learner activities. An ideal layout is to have the computers around the outside walls of the class – allowing you to view what is on each screen and to help should the need arise – and a central table where learners can congregate for more communicative activities. This table will also serve as a storage place for pens, books and dictionaries, and thus help keep the computers free of clutter and easy to use.

6 Not all of the content that you come across with your learners will necessarily be suitable for them. The wonder of the Internet is that it caters for a wide variety of people, interests and tastes, so much so that you are almost bound to encounter what you consider to be questionable content at some point in your exploration, and the same can safely be said of your learners. We have generally found an open discussion about the kind of things the group considers acceptable in class has been enough to put an end to any further unsuitable exploration, but if you work in a context where this is likely to be a bigger issue then you may need to take more robust steps such as installing filtering software along the lines of Net Nanny (www.netnanny.com), which will limit access to a wide range of content which can be user-specified and controlled.

Bearing in mind all these suggestions – and taking into account the successful combination of these searching, evaluating and planning skills – you should now be in a position to fully explore the web with your learners.

Conclusions | *In this chapter we have:*

- considered the difference between EFL-related and authentic websites.
- looked at how to find websites using different types of search engine.
- considered how to evaluate a website for classroom use.
- looked at lesson planning using Internet resources, at both higher and lower levels.
- provided a list of Internet teaching dos and don'ts.

ON THE CD-ROM YOU CAN HEAR THREE TEACHERS TALKING ABOUT USING WEBSITES.

 | **Internet-based project work**

- Why do Internet-based project work?
- Basic projects
- Internet-based simulations
- Webquests
- Webquest creation

Why do Internet-based project work?

A natural progression from using individual web pages and websites in the classroom is to move on to online project work. This will be an extension of the kind of individual-lesson work we have looked at in Chapter 3 and will involve the use of the Internet over a series of lessons. There are many compelling reasons for using Internet-based projects in the classroom:

1 They are a structured way for teachers to begin to incorporate the Internet into the language classroom, on both a short-term and a long-term basis. No specialist technical knowledge is needed either to produce or to use Internet-based projects. However, it is certainly true that they will take time to plan and design, so it is well worth looking around on the Internet to see if something appropriate already exists before sitting down to create your own project.

2 More often than not, they are group activities and, as a result, lend themselves to communication and the sharing of knowledge, two principal goals of language teaching itself. The use of projects encourages cooperative learning, and therefore stimulates interaction.

3 They can be used simply for language learning purposes, but can also be interdisciplinary, allowing for cross-over into other departments and subject areas. This can often give them a more 'real-world' look and feel, and provide greater motivation for the learner.

4 They encourage critical thinking skills. Learners are not required to simply regurgitate information they find, but have to transform that information in order to achieve a given task.

In the context of doing project work, the Internet can be thought of as an enormous encyclopedia because it gives our learners quick access to a wealth of information which they can use to carry out their project tasks. A good example of such a source is Wikipedia (www.wikipedia.org), a collaborative encyclopedia produced by and for the Internet community. Wikipedia has thousands of articles on many different subjects, and is an ideal place to start when doing project work that requires factual information about people and places. We will be examining Wikipedia and other online reference tools in greater detail in Chapter 8.

Project work online can range from a simple low-level project like making a poster presentation about a famous person to high-level investigative work where learners research a subject and present polemical views and opinions in a report or debate. In order to prepare for Internet-based project work, you will need to do the following:

- **Choose the project topic**
  Will your learners be researching famous people, an event or an issue?

- **Make the task clear**
  What information will they need to find – biographical, factual, views and opinions?

- **Find the resources**
  Which websites will your learners need to visit? Do these websites contain the information they need and are they at the right level? Refer back to Chapter 3 for more ideas on selecting and evaluating websites.

- **Decide on the outcome**
  What is the final purpose of the project? For example, will your learners be making a poster, a presentation or holding a debate?

Basic projects

A low-level project – My favourite actor

For this project you will need:

- three lesson periods of at least 45 minutes each (two if the first lesson is done for homework).
- access to the Internet for the second and third of the three suggested lessons.
- word processing software such as Microsoft Word or OpenOffice.

This is a common topic for project work, but our experience has been that learners rarely know more than the basics about their favourite actor, pop star or sports personality and certainly not usually enough for a full project. This is where the Internet comes into its own, providing the information they will need to fill the gaps in their knowledge.

This particular project aims to provide the opportunity to focus on these language areas: countries, nationalities, dates, places, past tenses, likes and dislikes, and opinions. During the project, learners research their favourite actor and prepare a poster presentation about them. This is also an ideal opportunity to tie in some of the skills we have covered both in Chapter 2 (word processing) and in Chapter 3 (searching and using websites), showing your learners the real value of acquiring these skills.

First lesson

If you are short of class time, a good deal of this first lesson can be done for homework and then finished off with the collaborative element in the second lesson. Be careful, however, to emphasise that what you are looking for at this stage is what they already know, and that they do not need to go to the Internet for any information at all.

Have your learners write down the name of their favourite actor and mind-map what they know about him or her. Use the following as a guide:

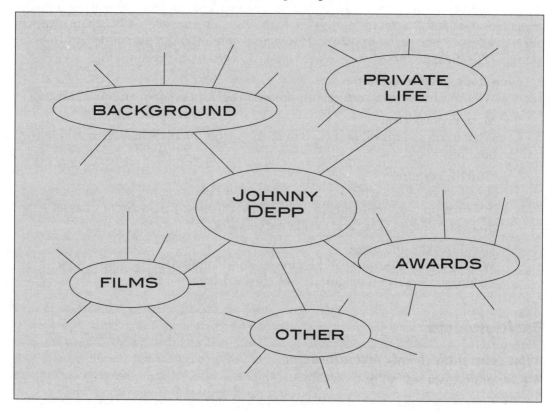

Once they have written down what they know, have them make a list of things they don't know, but would like to find out.

Second lesson

This second lesson requires a fair bit of work on the part of you, the teacher. If you think you may be short of time, limit the names of actors in the first lesson to a small selection that you have already researched.

Before the lesson you will need to find useful sites to match the choice of actors your learners made. Make sure that they are simple enough for the level, and include as much of the information sought as possible. You can use the skills you acquired in Chapter 3 to accomplish this. Remember that for biographical information you can search using a part phrase such as "*Johnny Depp was born in*". Alternatively, and if your learners are comfortable with searching and dealing with websites, have them find their own. In this lesson, your learners will visit the identified sites and complete their mind-map, as far as possible.

In the next stage, you will need to provide them with a model biography. Check out Wikipedia for examples (e.g. http://en.wikipedia.org/wiki/Johnny_Depp) and rewrite one example to your students' language level. You may decide to do some comprehension work on your model text at this time, working on the structures and vocabulary areas that you want them to include in their biographies.

Third lesson

This third lesson involves making the final product. By now your learners will have collected all the information they need and will also have seen your model biography, so they should be in a position to come up with one of their own.

One way of doing this is to have them prepare a short text based on the model from the previous lesson, and then to work this up into a poster (using Microsoft Word or similar) with illustrations and photographs also taken from the Internet. Remember that you can use http://images.google.com for relevant images.

Please remember that much of what you find on the Internet will be copyright material, so please ensure that you check that you are able to use the information and images you find. In the education field this is not normally a problem – 'fair use' of copyright materials is flexible when it comes to classroom use and a picture or two from a site such as Google will be acceptable as long as you keep the materials in the classroom or your learners' homes and they are not published anywhere. When in doubt, however, it is best to email the owner of the site you are using to check that they do not mind. Their final projects might look something like this:

Elementary

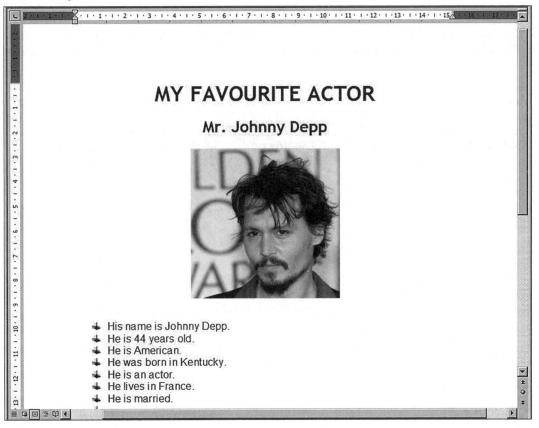

A high-level project – Global warming

This project aims to provide learners with the opportunity of examining a serious issue in depth. You may want to work beforehand on some of the language areas useful for the activity, for example giving opinions, agreeing and disagreeing. However, this will depend on the level of your learners. It is ideal for groups at an upper-intermediate level and above.

While the lower-level project we have just looked at is an ideal opportunity for developing specific communication skills, this project goes deeper into a topic and encourages more complex thinking and reasoning processes. With higher-level projects like this one there is plenty of opportunity for cross-curricular applications, working with teachers in other departments where possible, and for covering other areas of the overall syllabus above and beyond the teaching of English. For this project you will need:

- three lesson periods of at least 45 minutes each.

- access to the Internet for the first and possibly second of the three suggested lessons.

- optionally, access to video recording equipment for the third lesson.

First lesson

This lesson can easily be done in 45 minutes, but learners would benefit from more time for their research into the topic and for the subsequent discussion of their findings, if that time is available.

Brainstorm what your learners know about global warming. Use this chart as a starting point:

Global warming				
Evidence for	Evidence against	Countries involved	Possible effects	Possible solutions

Now divide them into five groups, one for each topic in the table above. Take them to http://en.wikipedia.org/wiki/Global_warming as a starting point, and give them time to add to their column. They may also use their own search skills to find out more, if there is time. Return to whole class discussion, and discuss the contents of the refined table.

Second lesson

This second lesson will also fit into a 45-minute period, but again the depth and quality of their preparation will improve if they are given more time. Since in the third lesson they will be role-playing a television debate, you might also like to encourage them to think about how they can enhance the final product with, for example, the use of props and arrangement of the furniture.

Divide the class into four groups, working towards a special television debate on global warming:

- TV debate presenters.
- scientists who deny that global warming exists, or that it is potentially dangerous.
- environmental campaigners wanting to inform the public of the dangers.
- TV studio audience.

In the third lesson you will have the actual debate, so now they must prepare their section of the debate.

- **Presenters**
  Decide which areas you want to cover in the televised debate. Who will speak first? How long will they speak for? Will interruptions and questions be permitted and how will you manage them? What questions will you need to ask? How will you deal with difficult speakers, or members of the public? Will you need any visual aids for your introduction?

- **Scientists**
  Look back at what your group discovered in the 'evidence against' column of the global warming table in the last lesson. It's your job to convince the studio audience, and the viewing public, that global warming does not really exist, and is certainly not dangerous. Your view is that it is a naturally occurring phenomenon and not man-made. Decide on your arguments, and prepare any visual elements you may need to illustrate your points.

- **Environmentalists**
  Look back at what your group discovered in the 'evidence for' and 'countries involved' columns of the global warming table in the last lesson. It's your job to convince the studio audience, and the viewing public, that global warming does exist, and is definitely dangerous. Your view is that it is man-made, and the product of certain countries. Decide on your arguments, and prepare any visual elements you may need to illustrate them.

- **Studio audience**
  You may decide individually on your views of global warming, based on what you found out in the last lesson – look back at the global warming table for a reminder. If you decide that you do not believe in global warming, prepare a couple of questions or statements to support the scientists (evidence against). If you opt to support the environmentalists, prepare a couple of questions or statements in their favour. If you adopt a more pragmatic view, that (rather than worrying about the cause and whose fault it is) we should instead be looking at ways of dealing with rising global temperatures (possible solutions), then prepare a couple of questions for that standpoint.

Each group should now prepare their role, doing further research if necessary, and preparing charts and other visual aids if they will be of help to them.

Third lesson

Here your learners will have the actual debate. If it is possible, simulate a TV studio in your classroom by moving the tables and chairs around, creating spaces for the four groups and encouraging your learners to decorate them. If they have props, arrange everything and prepare for the programme.

The presenters will be in charge of the debate, and ultimately responsible for what happens. If you have access to a video camera, you may want to record it for later playback. It can be particularly valuable for examining the language used in the process and for error correction. A simple home video camera should suffice, but ensure that lighting in the room is adequate for filming, and encourage everyone to speak as clearly as possible to achieve good audio quality. That is more important than the quality of the video. If you're already adept at video editing, take the programme home and add some titles and music to end up with a polished production.

Make sure that the stages of debate do not overrun. The worst thing that can happen is that you run out of time to conclude the debate properly.

Internet-based simulations

Internet-based simulations bring real-life contexts to the classroom, helping our learners to deal with situations that they may come across during foreign travel or in encounters with other speakers of English. The more traditional approach has teachers cutting up prepared role-cards in order to simulate these contexts. The Internet largely does away with this approach, giving learners access to authentic websites that provide stimulating and relevant content that enables them to carry out these simulations. Simulations like these work particularly well in the field of business English, where the language learning is very task- or goal-oriented, but they also work well with general English learners who may have less clearly defined reasons for using English, as we will see below.

A business English simulation

This sample simulation looks at the case of a personal assistant having to organise their manager's business trip to the United Kingdom. The benefit of this kind of simulation is that it uses real websites, and a potentially real situation, to further the learner's reading, information processing, planning and communication skills. As an additional benefit, it also addresses technology skills that are useful in this professional context.

Of course, a busy teacher is not going to prepare complex simulations such as this on a daily basis, but for occasional activities they really can bring home not only how useful the Internet is for busy professional people, but can also be an important confidence booster for learners. Working through carefully guided but complex tasks such as these – tasks which have a direct relation to what they do in their work – can reinforce the value of their language classes and keep motivation high.

In this particular simulation, we take the case of a learner who communicates primarily in the written form, using letters, faxes and emails. It is this factor that influences the nature of the tasks in the simulation (see opposite).

Situation

Your boss works for the Barcelona office of Candlewhite Consulting and has to go to the United Kingdom at the end of the month. The meeting itinerary has been prepared by your company's head office in London, but the logistics of the trip have been left to you. Look at your boss's itinerary below.

It's your responsibility to get your boss to each meeting on time, organising travel tickets and itineraries, and to arrange suitable accommodation for each night. For each day, organise transport allowing your boss to get to the meetings on time, and a good hotel to rest in at the end of the day. Remember, she's a heavy smoker and she needs Internet access in her hotel room. The following websites will help you:

Travel
- http://thetrainline.com
- http://www.opodo.co.uk/
- http://www.aferry.to/stranraer-ferry.htm

Accommodation
- http://www.hotels-london.co.uk/
- http://www.manchesteronline.co.uk/hotels/
- http://www.glasgowguide.co.uk/hotels.html
- http://belfast.gtahotels.com/
- http://www.city-visitor.com/bristol/hotels.html

Itinerary – Sra Irina Tarrejas
Primary office visits

Date	Morning	Afternoon	Evening
11	10:00–12:00 Briefing, London office	12:00–14:00 Lunch, Directors	19:00 Dinner, Manchester office
12	10:00–13:00 Briefing, Manchester office	16:00–17:00 Afternoon tea, Liverpool branch	20:00 Manchester Opera House – Rocky Horror Show
13	09:30–11:30 Briefing, Glasgow office	13:00–15:00 Lunch, Glasgow office	FREE TIME
14	11:00–13:00 Briefing, Belfast office	FREE TIME	20:00 Dinner meeting, Bristol office

You will need to find flights, trains or ferries and to work out which is the best way of getting from meeting to meeting. Note down prices and timetables. For accommodation, check online booking forms to ensure that rooms are available, and also note down the cost. You may also need to email to ensure late check-ins, early check-outs and other specifics such as smoking rooms and Internet access. Fill in the chart on page 52 as you get the information.

Date	Morning	Afternoon	Evening
10		Flight: Barcelona–London Flight number: Departure time: Arrival time: Price:	London hotel Hotel name: Address: Booking name: Price:
11		Transport: London–Manchester Type: Departure time/place: Arrival time: Price:	Manchester hotel (2 nights) Hotel name: Address: Booking name: Price:
12		Transport: Manchester–Liverpool Type: Departure time/place: Arrival time: Price:	Transport: Liverpool–Manchester Type: Departure time/place: Arrival time: Price:
13	Transport: Manchester–Glasgow Type: Departure time/place: Arrival time: Price:		Transport: Glasgow–Belfast Type: Departure time/place: Arrival time: Price: Belfast hotel: Hotel name: Address: Booking name: Price:
14		Transport: Belfast–Bristol Type: Departure time/place: Arrival time: Price: Bristol hotel: Hotel name: Address: Booking name: Price:	
15	Transport: Bristol–London Type: Departure time/place: Arrival time: Price:	Flight: London–Barcelona Flight number: Departure time: Arrival time:	
			Total cost:

When you have all the information you need, prepare a written report for your boss, detailing the complete itinerary, including all travel, accommodation, meeting and entertainment information.

A general English simulation

As observed above, simulations need to address potential real-life situations in order to appeal to the learner. The business-oriented example above is a clear case of this approach, but how can this kind of activity be prepared for learners of general English?

The activity above could easily be adapted for a more general context by turning it into a holiday being planned by a group of friends, or even a school trip. In this context, small groups would plan an itinerary around the United Kingdom, researching travel options, accommodation and things to do in each place visited. This might be presented as an award given to the students, with a limited budget, making the actual logistics more challenging, but more real. Shorter simulations are also possible, as in this example.

Situation

As chairperson of the student committee you have been nominated to present the student awards this year. Your job is to propose the prizes to be given, and to arrange for them to be bought and delivered. There are three prizes:

- Best student – €300 prize money
  winner: Francine Dumas, 17 – interests: computers, science.
- Best volunteer – €250 prize money
  winner: Pawel Krajka, 15 – interests: the environment, hiking, travel.
- Best sporting achievement – €200 prize money
  winner: Pablo Castro, 16 – interests: extreme sports, climbing, camping.

Your committee has decided to buy the prizes online. Visit the following online shopping sites and find three possible prizes for each person.

- http://www.amazon.co.uk
- http://www.pcworld.co.uk
- http://www.dell.co.uk
- http://www.expedia.co.uk
- http://www.opodo.co.uk
- http://www.extremepie.com
- http://www.simplyhike.co.uk
- http://www.blacks.co.uk
- http://www.gear-zone.co.uk
- http://www.ecoshop.com.au

Complete this chart. Remember to include a picture of each potential prize, as well as the site it is available from and the price.

Person	Suggestion 1	Suggestion 2	Suggestion 3
Francine			
Pawel			
Pablo			

Now write a short report for the committee, explaining the three possible choices for each person and making a personal recommendation about which one you feel should be bought. Include your chart.

Webquests

Webquests are mini-projects in which a large percentage of the input and material is supplied from the Internet. Webquests can be teacher-made or learner-made, depending on the learning activity the teacher decides on. What makes webquests different from projects or simulations is the fairly rigid structure they have evolved over the years, and it is this structure – and the process of implementing webquests in the classroom – that we will be exploring here.

Bernie Dodge, a Professor of Educational Technology at San Diego State University, was one of the first people to attempt to define and structure this kind of learning activity. According to him, a webquest is 'an inquiry-oriented activity in which some or all of the information that learners interact with comes from resources on the Internet'. He goes on to identify two types of webquest:

- **Short-term webquests**
  At the end of a short-term webquest, a learner will have grappled with a significant amount of new information and made sense of it. A short-term webquest may spread over a period of a couple of classes or so, and will involve learners in visiting a selection of sites to find information, and using that information in class to achieve a set of learning aims.

- **Longer-term webquests**
  After completing a longer-term webquest, a learner will have analysed a body of knowledge deeply, transforming it in some way. They will have demonstrated an understanding of the material by creating something that others can respond to, online or offline. This is the big difference between the longer-term and short-term webquests – learners have to transform the information they acquire, turning it into a new product: a report, a presentation, an interview or a survey. Longer-term webquests might last a few weeks, or even a term or semester.

Webquests have now been around long enough for them to have a clearly-defined structure. However, this structure, while being unofficially recognised as the definitive schema for these activities, should only really be taken as a basic guideline and you should design your webquests to suit the needs and learning styles of your group. In the example, we will be examining an ELT webquest about responsible consumerism. It is designed for intermediate-level learners. There are usually four main sections to a webquest:

Step 1 – Introduction

This stage is normally used to introduce the overall theme of the webquest. It involves giving background information on the topic and, in the language learning context, often introduces key vocabulary and concepts which learners will need to understand in order to complete the tasks involved.

In the example opposite, learners are introduced to the idea of responsible consumerism by considering various scenarios relevant to their own circumstances.

1 Introduction

Step 2 – Task

The **task** section of the webquest explains clearly and precisely what the learners will have to do as they work their way through the webquest. The task should obviously be highly motivating and intrinsically interesting for the learners, and should be firmly anchored in a real-life situation. This often involves the learners in a certain amount of role-play within a given scenario, as in the example, 'You are a team of investigative reporters'.

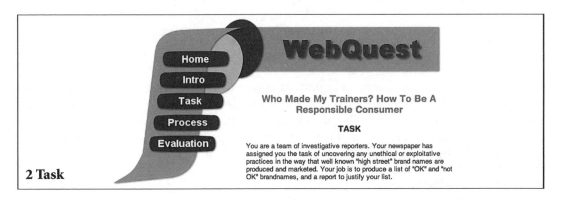

2 Task

Step 3 – Process

The **process** stage of a webquest guides the learners through a set of activities and research tasks, using a set of predefined resources.

These resources are predominantly Internet-based, and are usually presented in clickable form, that is, as a set of active links to websites within the task document. It's important to bear in mind that it's much easier to click on a link than to type it in with any degree of accuracy.

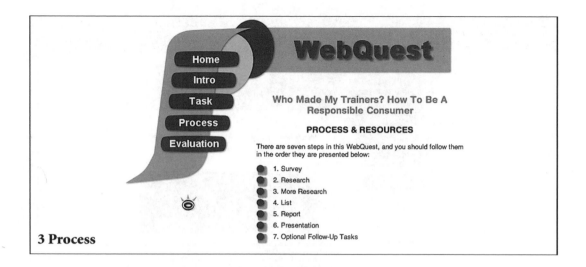

3 Process

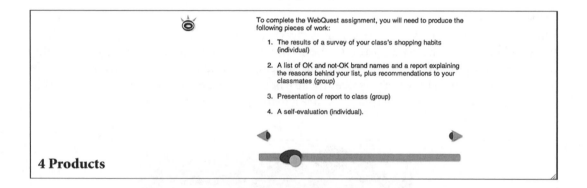

4 Products

In the case of a language-based webquest, as opposed to a purely content-based one, the process stage of the webquest may introduce or recycle lexical areas or grammatical points which are essential to the task. The process stage of the webquest will usually have one or sometimes several 'products' which the learners are expected to present at the end. These 'products' will often form the basis of the evaluation stage.

Step 4 – Evaluation

The **evaluation** stage can involve learners in self-evaluation, comparing and contrasting what they have produced with other learners, and giving feedback on what they feel they have learnt and achieved.

It will also involve teacher evaluation, and good webquests will give guidance to the teacher for this particular part of the process. Since Bernie Dodge developed his model in 1995, many educators have added both to the theory and the practice of webquests, and it is now possible to find several good examples of them in many different subject areas.

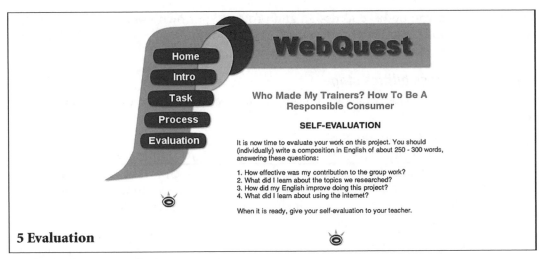

5 Evaluation

Webquest creation

Creating a webquest does not require much detailed technical knowledge. It is relatively easy to produce a professional-looking and workable design using any modern word processor. The skillset for producing a webquest is very similar to what we explored earlier for planning Internet-based lessons, and might be defined as follows:

- **Research skills** (see Chapter 3)
  It is essential to be able to search the Internet and to quickly and accurately find resources. The best search engines currently available are Google (www.google.com) for wide searches over a large database of websites and Yahoo! (www.yahoo.com) for a more theme-based approach.

- **Analytical skills** (see Chapter 3)
  It is also very important to be able to cast a critical eye over the resources you do find when searching. The Internet was once described as 'vanity publishing gone mad', and it is worth bearing in mind that quality is not guaranteed. Make sure to check out any website you are considering using thoroughly before basing any activity around it. Simply because the author of a website believes elephants to be bulletproof – a real example – doesn't mean that they really are.

- **Word processing skills** (see Chapter 2)
  You will also need to be able to use a word processor to combine text, images and weblinks into a finished document. This particular set of skills can be acquired quickly and easily.

Before sitting down to plan a webquest – as noted at the start of this chapter – it is always worth searching around on the Internet to see if someone has produced something which might fit your needs. There are plenty of webquest 'repositories', so there is little point in reinventing the wheel. Use Google to have a good look round before you do the hard work yourself – try a search for ELT webquests – or start with one of these sites:

- http://www.webquest.org
- http://www.fi.muni.cz/ICT4ELT/websites/webquests_nepouzivase.html
- http://www.theconsultants-e.com/webquests/

In the event that you do have to design and produce your own webquest, Tom March, a colleague of Bernie Dodge, has produced a flow chart for the design process, which you can see opposite. Let's examine how the process works.

Exploring the possibilities stage

In this section we decide what we're going to base our webquest on, and start to find resources.

- **Choose and chunk the topic**
  The first thing to do is to decide on a macro (or large) topic and then break it down into micro (smaller) chunks of topic areas which will be addressed in the process stages of the webquest. In our example, the macro topic is 'responsible consumerism', the micro topics include: animal testing, child labour, sexism, ethical production and marketing.

- **Identify learning gaps**
  As we have seen, webquests are good for dealing with critical thinking skills, problem solving and group dynamics. Identify which areas your learners would benefit from, and design tasks for the process stage accordingly. The sample webquest we have been looking at has a wide variety of personal interactions and content interactions designed to activate critical thinking skills and encourage collaborative work.

- **Inventory resources**
  This involves collecting the resources for the webquest, including links to appropriate websites, images with which to decorate the webquest and media files. You will need to find all this before you move on to the design process.

- **Uncover the question**
  In this stage, you need to ensure that you have a central question or idea which has no single answer, and which necessitates research and interpretation. This is the central purpose of the webquest. In our example, the introduction states 'you will investigate the way your favourite brands – of clothes, fast food, cosmetics, etc – are produced and marketed, with a view to becoming better informed and therefore a more discriminating consumer'. This, then, is the 'question' – and it is something that your learners should be interested in, but not have fully formed ideas about.

Designing for success stage

In this stage, we further structure the webquest and ensure that the learning outcomes and knowledge transformation stages are clearly delineated.

- **Brainstorm transformations**
  This involves deciding what your learners will be doing with the information they find on the websites. Bernie Dodge identified this stage as what happens between 'learning inputs' and 'learning outcomes'. This is where you flesh out the tasks in the process stage, guiding your learners through the information they uncover, and helping them towards an understanding and transformation of that information as they work towards the products they need to put together.

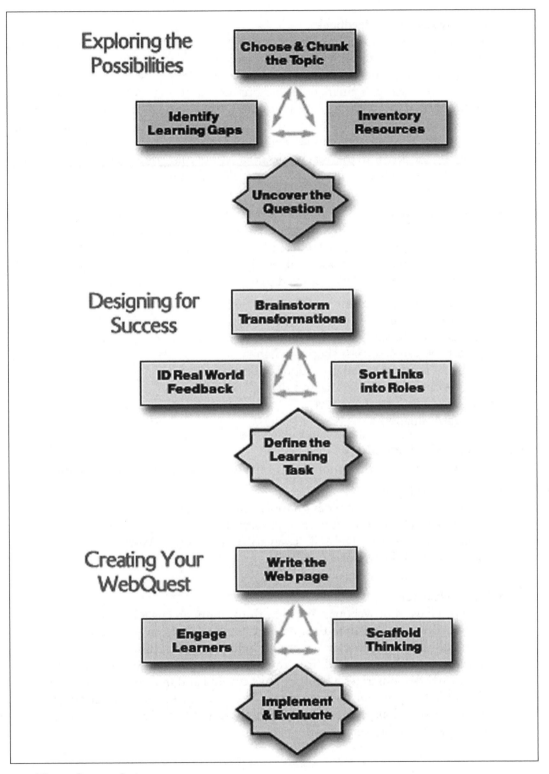

The webquest design process

- **Identify real-world feedback**
  Tom March feels that learners should be engaged with the wider world when they are working with webquests. This means that you might try looking for ways in which the information necessary for the webquest might be gathered from real people – by the use of email, polls and questionnaires. This can also be 'offline', in the sense of interviewing colleagues, staff, friends and family. In our example, learners conduct a class survey on their favourite brands – and this could perhaps be extended through the school, or put online as an electronic survey, thus widening the access to the 'real world'. In a school this would involve interviewing other classes, while an online survey can quickly be put together using a tool such as Survey Monkey (www.surveymonkey.com).

- **Sort links into roles**
  The links you identified in the inventory resources section should now be assigned to the various sections of the process stage of your webquest, ensuring that the websites are easily navigable, understandable and contain the information that your learners need to work through the webquest.

- **Define the learning task**
  This refers to the products which are the direct result of working through the webquest. In the sample we have looked at, learners have to produce:
  - a survey results of class shopping habits.
  - a list of acceptable and unacceptable brands.
  - a report to the class on the brands.
  - a presentation of the report.
  - a self-evaluation.

Creating your webquest stage

In this stage, we move on to the production of the webquest and its implementation.

- **Write the web page**
  If you're familiar with web design tools you will be able to turn your webquest plan into a website and put it on a web server. But this is, perhaps, a slow way of preparing a webquest. The easiest way to do this is to use Word, adding links to each section of the webquest, some images to liven up the material and the links to the resources your learners will visit.

- **Engage learners**
  Now you have your webquest in place, think about an engaging and stimulating introduction as a lead-in to the quest itself. Hopefully your webquest will have plenty of motivating tasks and websites in it, so the final thing that you need to do is to get learners involved from the outset, and to draw them to a conclusion that clearly demonstrates what they have covered and that rounds the quest off satisfactorily. In our sample, learners are invited to consider a variety of consumer situations in the introduction phase and to evaluate their learning and participation in the conclusion.

- **Scaffold thinking**
  In this stage you need to think about the instructions given in the webquest itself. These instructions should not only guide the learners through the webquest, but should also deal with the learning gap identified in the exploring the possibilities stage, and guide them towards answering the question. This will involve not only support in the content area but will also help with the language needed to carry out the webquest. Ensure that your learners have access to the language that they will need to use.

- **Decision: implement and evaluate**
  The final stage is to try out the webquest with a group or two, take feedback from them and also consider how it went for you, and make appropriate changes for future use.

Note that webquests can also be produced by learners as part of a more detailed and longer-term project. Often, this significant investment in the materials production side of the teaching/learning process is a highly motivating class activity in itself.

Conclusions | *In this chapter we have:*

- looked at extending Internet usage from the simple lesson plan described in Chapter 3 to more extensive project work, simulations and webquests.

- seen how the Internet can be used as an access point to real-world knowledge which our learners might lack.

- examined how the Internet can act as a springboard for authentic, relevant simulation work and as the source of materials which promote collaborative learning, communication, knowledge sharing and higher-level thinking skills.

- explored the area of motivation and considered how this can be increased with careful task design and judicious choice of Internet content.

- looked at the methodology for creating and using webquests.

> ON THE CD-ROM YOU CAN HEAR A TEACHER TALKING ABOUT DOING INTERNET-BASED PROJECT WORK WITH SECONDARY SCHOOL STUDENTS AND WATCH A TUTORIAL WHICH GIVES YOU MORE INFORMATION ABOUT THE 'WHO MADE MY TRAINERS?' WEBQUEST.

How to use email

- **The benefits of email**
- **Basic email skills**
- **Using email with learners out of class**
- **Using email with learners during class**
- **Keypal projects**

The benefits of email

Email is one of the most used and useful Information and Communication Technology (ICT) tools around today. Most of us probably write emails in both our personal and professional lives, and the same thing is true for many of our learners. Email allows us to keep in touch with other teachers around the world via **mailing lists** and **discussion groups**, thus helping in our professional development (see Chapter 11). It also allows us to communicate with our learners outside the classroom, for example setting, receiving, marking and returning homework and other written assignments.

Typically, email will be used outside class time. For example, learners will email work to their teacher or to other learners from their home or from an **Internet café**. However, in the case of keypal projects – email projects set up between learners in different classes or countries – and when learner access to computers outside the teaching institution is very limited, a school computer or computers may be used in class time very successfully.

Reading and writing emails either in or outside class time gives a learner more exposure to the target language, and interaction is 'real' in the sense that learners are writing to real people – either the teacher or other learners – using a 'real' medium. In addition, if learners are writing to learners in other countries, as in a keypal project, this allows them to make contact and interact with people with different first languages and from other cultures.

One of the biggest advantages of using email with learners from the teacher's point of view is that the technology is relatively simple to use, and most of our learners will already be familiar with it. If our learners are not familiar with email, it is not difficult to teach them to use it, and the technology is both ubiquitous and free.

Basic email skills

Before starting to use email with learners, you will need to check that your learners have certain basic skills in place. Learners need to be familiar not only with the mechanics of sending and receiving emails and attachments, but also with the kind of language used in email, as well as the 'rules of engagement', or **netiquette**, required in email use. Basic skills may be considered in two groups: communication skills and technical skills.

Communication skills

It is a good idea to remind learners that, as in traditional letter writing, there are levels of formality in email writing. An email written to enquire about a job vacancy will have a different level of formality to an email sent to a close friend. While the email to a friend may include abbreviations, emoticons, misspellings or lower-case characters such as *i*, these are entirely inappropriate for a more formal email. If you are using email with your learners – for example to receive homework – you will want to negotiate with them the level of formality you feel is acceptable. Probably you will apply the same criteria you would apply to a piece of written work on paper.

It is also a good idea to teach your learners some of the basics of netiquette. These are 'rules' for effective online communication. Well-known netiquette rules include:

- not using only capital letters, which is perceived as 'shouting' online.

- being sure to respect others' opinions.

- avoiding 'flaming' – ongoing arguments which become increasingly personalised and possibly public.

- making sure that files sent as email attachments are not too large, as the person receiving the email may not be able to download them.

Composing an email has the added advantage for learners of allowing them to draft and edit before sending. Research shows that this part of the writing process – so much easier than with pen and paper – is something that learners appreciate. But communication by email is, of course, still very fast.

Technical skills

Apart from basic word processing and typing skills, learners will need to have an email account. Many learners will already have a personal or work email account that they will be willing to use for their language classwork, but others may need help with setting up a new email account. There are several free, web-based email services, through which it is easy to set up and use an email account. The best known are Yahoo!, Hotmail or Google Mail, although Google Mail currently requires you to receive an invitation from an already registered Google Mail user for you to be able to open an account.

Once learners have their email accounts, they need to be able to send and receive email, and to attach and open documents in email. It is also useful for learners to have basic ICT skills, such as knowledge about viruses sent by email, and spam or unsolicited junk email – what these are, and how to protect themselves from them.

Depending on your teaching context, you may want to first give your learners a questionnaire to assess the overall email skills of the class, and then to review basic email skills based on the results of that survey, either with the whole class, with individual learners or by pairing up an experienced email user with a novice and asking the experienced user to teach the novice basic email skills outside class time. If the language level of the class is low, there is a case for providing this basic technical skills training in the learners' first language if you teach in a monolingual context.

On page 64 is a suggested questionnaire that you can adapt for use with your own learners, to gauge their level of skill in using email, as well as finding out about how much access to email they have, and what they know about viruses and spam. If the overall email skills of the class are low, you should leave out references to viruses and spam, and concentrate only on the most basic email skills of sending and receiving, and of sending and opening email attachments.

Email questionnaire	Yes	No
1 I have my own email account. (What email service do you use?)		
2 I use email at home.		
3 I use email at work/school.		
4 I have access to a computer at home.		
5 I know how to write, send and read emails.		
6 I know how to send an attachment by email.		
7 I know how to open an email attachment.		
8 I know what a virus is.		
9 I know what to do if I receive a virus by email.		
10 I know what 'spam' email is.		
11 I know how to receive less spam by email.		

Using email with learners out of class

There are many ways of using email with learners, from simple administrative tasks such as the submission of assignments or homework via email, to more complex email projects, involving classes in different countries over a number of weeks, a semester or even over an academic year. Below we outline some ideas for using email outside the classroom. The ideas require learners to have their own email accounts, and access to a computer outside class time, either at home or work, in a self-access centre, or in an Internet café.

- Learners can submit classwork as attachments by email, which can be marked by the teacher, and returned by email. Learners can also share classwork/assignments by email.

- The teacher can email learners a summary of classwork, plus homework or extra material, or updates on classes, after each class or on a regular (e.g. weekly) basis. A teacher blog can also work well for this (see Chapter 7).

- The teacher can email learners regular newsletters about the class and themselves. This is especially useful for keeping in touch with learners during holidays. The emails could include 'diary' or 'journal' type information about what the teacher has been doing in their spare time, and be sent to learners weekly, fortnightly or monthly. Learners can be encouraged to send each other emails of this type, too, either to the whole class, or to a partner.

- Learners can use email to prepare before class. For example, the teacher can ask pairs to prepare information on a topic, which they can do via email.

- Learners can use email to send queries about a topic, or a grammar area, to the teacher before a class. This can help the teacher prepare a class that focuses on and addresses specific learner issues.

- A class mailing list can be set up for general discussions out of class time. (See Chapter 11 for more on mailing lists.) Regular email programs can also be used for this, with learners simply setting up a class group in their email program address books.

- Email can be used as a collaborative writing tool. For example, in groups, learners are asked to produce a story based on a painting, with Learner 1 starting the story, which is then forwarded to Learner 2, who adds to the story, then forwards it to Learner 3, who adds to it, and so on. It is important to ensure that all group members are copied into the story from the beginning, and that each learner knows when it is their turn to contribute! Note that a wiki can also work well for collaborative writing (see Chapter 7).

Using email with learners during class

Using email during class time is worth doing if more complex projects are being set up and if your learners have limited access to computers outside the classroom. Below we describe two examples of data collection projects. These can run over several classes, weeks or even months, and require quite a lot preparation on the part of the teacher.

A data collection project requires learners to send emails to real companies, individuals, organisations or websites to solicit information. This information is then collated for comparison, and a presentation or written report is prepared on the topic. Given that the chances of unsolicited emails not being answered is high, it's important to ensure that you choose a topic that requires your learners to send emails that stand a good chance of receiving a response.

Here are two example data collection projects for learners with an intermediate or higher level of English. Given that emails for data collection projects need to be written with a fair degree of accuracy, they are less suitable for low levels.

Data collection project 1: Language courses in Australia	
Theme	language learning, study abroad, travel, cultures
Aim	to collate information about English language courses in Australia
Learners	adult learners, intermediate and higher levels
Suggested time frame	2 lessons of 60 to 90 minutes each
Procedure	
Lesson 1	**a** The teacher provides pairs of learners with one language school website each in Australia (or another English-speaking country). These schools can be in one geographical area, e.g. New South Wales or Queensland, or all over Australia.
	b Pairs visit the website, read the information available, find an email address for further enquiries and compile a series of questions to email to the school about the language course on offer. These might include asking for further information about accommodation, transport, local sights, attractions and activities, food, fees and course content.

	c Pairs write an email, which can then be checked by another pair and/or the teacher, and send it to the language school. To minimise the risk of learners not receiving an answer to their enquiry, the teacher can supply each pair with two websites to write to.
Lesson 2	**d** Once all of the pairs have received an answer to their enquiries, learners are regrouped to share what they have found out. Each new group decides which course they think is the 'best' and why. If one pair is without an email reply, the pair can be split up and each learner join a pair who has received a reply, to help them with their presentation.
	e Follow-up activities might include a spoken presentation on each language course to the class, or a written report, or findings can be presented using other ICT tools such as a blog, or a podcast (see Chapter 7).

Data collection project 2: Endangered animals	
Theme	endangered species, ecology
Aim	to find out about endangered species
Learners	adolescent (aged 14+) and adult learners, intermediate and higher levels
Suggested time frame	2 to 3 lessons of 60 to 90 minutes each
Procedure	
Lesson 1	**a** The teacher provides pairs of learners with one website each, which deals with animals in danger of extinction. Example websites are: The World Wildlife Fund, Greenpeace, the Sumatran Orangutan Society, the Cheetah Conservation Fund, the Gorilla Fund and Save the Whale. A search in Google for 'endangered species' or similar will bring up a wealth of links. You can give each pair a site dedicated to one specific animal in danger of extinction.
	b Pairs visit the website, read the information available, find an email address for further enquiries and compile a series of questions to email to the organisation. The email might include asking for further information about the animal in question and about awareness raising techniques, as well as a request for promotional material from the organisation such as posters, slides, brochures, membership forms or car stickers.
	c Pairs write an email containing compiled questions, which can then be checked by another pair and/or the teacher, and send it to the organisation.
Lesson 2	**d** Once all the pairs have received an answer to their enquiries, they prepare a written or oral presentation to share what they have found out about 'their' animal with the rest of the class, and to display any promotional material they have received.

Lesson 3	e Follow-up activities might include new groups preparing the overall findings about all the endangered animals researched, which can be presented using other ICT tools such as a blog, a wiki or a podcast. A school awareness raising day/morning can also be arranged with student-made posters and promotional materials put on display.

Keypal projects

Keypals is the term for pen pals who use email to communicate, and described below is a project between two groups of keypals who are learning English in different countries. Email provides a simple and effective way of putting learners in touch with other learners of the same age and level in other parts of the world. Learners can talk about their experiences of learning English, and, of course, email is the perfect medium for cross-cultural communication. Keypal projects should be started in class but thereafter could combine a mixture of in-class and out-of-class work.

Keypal project: Learners around the world	
Theme	learning English, other countries and cultures
Aim	to find out about another country and what it's like learning English there
Learners	young learners (aged 12+) and adult learners, elementary level and higher
Suggested time frame	5 lessons of 1 hour each
Procedure	
Before starting the project	a Contact a teacher in another country with a similar class via email. The easiest way to find another teacher is via an online professional development group. (See Chapter 11 for more information about making contact with other teachers.)
	b Exchange detailed information about your classes – number of learners, level of English, interests and ages.
	c Decide exactly how you will pair up your learners with the other teacher's learners. Who will work with whom?
	d Decide whether pairs will be using their own email accounts, or one main class email account – for example the teacher's email. This latter option works well for the single computer classroom.
	e Decide on a time frame. When exactly will the first email be sent? When will a reply email be sent? For this project, you will need five one-hour classes.
	f Compile a short list of websites which contain the information that your learners will need to complete the pre-project work below.
Lesson 1	a **Pairwork using the Internet.** Tell your learners that they will be contacting learners in another country. First, they will need to find out some basic information about that country.
	b As a class, brainstorm what learners already know about the country, and put it on the board.
	c Divide the class into small groups so that each group has access to a computer.

	d Give each group a topic to research (e.g. geography, typical food, languages, tourist attractions), and provide each group with a website address where they can find this information. Give them a time limit (e.g. 10 minutes) to find out as much as they can.
	e Regroup the learners to share what they have found out. Now each of these groups needs to write two or three more questions that they would like to ask someone who lives in the other country.
Lesson 2	**a** **Writing an introductory email.** Tell your learners the name of the keypal they will be sending their email to. Learners (individually or in pairs) compose an email to this keypal, including the following information: • introduce yourself (name, age, gender, interests). • describe what it's like living in your country. • describe what it's like learning English in your country (number of hours per week, types of activities, what you like/don't like about your English classes, how much English is present – or not – outside the classroom, e.g. subtitled films, TV, magazines). • include the questions from the pre-project phase above. As this email is a first draft, it can be done either on paper, or more effectively in a word processing program.
	b **Checking and revising the emails.** Learners now exchange their draft email with another student in the same class for checking. As the email will be sent to another country and to someone they don't yet know, learners are usually very keen for their email to be as 'correct' as possible.
	c Learners give feedback to each other on their emails.
	d Learners correct/revise their email until they are satisfied that it is ready to be sent.
	e Learners send the email to their keypal. Note: It is important that you have previously agreed a timeframe with the other teacher in the project. Learners should receive an introductory email from their keypal in time for the next class.
Lesson 3	**a** Learners receive and read their emails.
	b Learners write a short reply thanking their keypal, and answering the questions in the email. Again, learners spend time in class checking and revising their emails before sending.
Lesson 4	**a** Learners receive and read their second emails.
	b In small groups, they need to prepare a poster or presentation describing what they have learnt about the other country. They need to include two main sections: • what they have learnt about the country itself. • what they have learnt about learning English in that country. Give learners class time to prepare their poster/presentation. You may want to allow them to download photos from the Internet sites in the pre-project phase to decorate their posters. Allow them some rehearsal time.
Lesson 5	**a** Learners in their small groups now present their poster/findings to the class. If you have very large classes, you could divide the learners into two large groups, so that you have two presentations happening simultaneously.
	b At the end of all the presentations, you could have the class vote 'prizes' for whose presentation was the most: • full of facts. • visually attractive. • amusingly presented. • well researched. Make sure that there is a prize category for all of the presentations.

Suggested follow-up activities	**a** Information on what learners have found out about the other country can be presented using other ICT tools such as a blog, a wiki or a podcast, and shared with the keypals. The initial email contact established by a keypal project such as this also provides a good base on which to build more complex follow-up projects using tools such as blogs and wikis.
	b A 'culture box' of real objects can be posted to the partner class, and might include audio tapes of favourite English songs, advertising from magazines, food labels containing English and photos of the group. This simply makes the partner groups more 'real' to each other.

Keypal projects issues

Here is a checklist of things to bear in mind when planning a keypal project. Some points have already been mentioned.

- Ensure that you agree on clear deadlines and time frames with your partner teacher for emails to arrive, and stick to these. There is nothing more demotivating for learners than to put in the effort of writing emails, and to then get no response, or a slow response.

- Negotiate groupings with your partner teacher, and decide whether emails will be written by individuals in one class to individuals in the other class, in pairs or in groups, or even as a whole class (good for very low levels).

- Decide which languages will be used in emails, depending on who the learners involved are. For example, if both classes are learning English as a foreign language, with one class in Chile, and the other in Germany, English will be used for all of the emails. If one class is native speaker, then it's worth trying to pair up the languages – for example, a group of English-speaking learners in the UK studying German with a group of German-speaking learners in Germany studying English. In this way, half of each email can be written in one language (German) and half in the other (English), with learners writing partly in their mother tongue and partly in the target language, which can feel less threatening. This kind of exchange is easiest to set up at secondary school level.

- Ensure that all learners have the basic emailing skills and knowledge of email netiquette outlined earlier in this chapter.

- Keep the keypal project short and focused. The keypal project outlined above runs over five classes. Ensure that your learners know how long the project is to last, and when it will be finished by – don't let things drag on. Focus is provided by having clear tasks for each email, as in the outline above. Don't expect learners to simply write an email to a stranger without any guidance as to content or language.

- Discuss with your partner teacher to what extent there will be teacher involvement. Will the teacher vet and approve each email, and to what extent will accuracy and 'correct' language be an issue? This also needs to be made clear to learners, especially if their emails are to be used in any sort of assessment procedures.

- Discuss with your learners the issue of possible misunderstandings across cultures. For example, do emails come across as too direct or blunt? Do they sound rude? If so, what might cause this, and what writing conventions do we need to use in English to avoid this? Responding to email using the reader's first name, for example, and signing off in a friendly fashion, is important. Again, this relates to the area of netiquette.

- In terms of general email etiquette in email projects, it is worth reminding learners that it is always a good idea to remain polite, and to not respond to aggressive or insulting emails – although this is unlikely to be a problem if a keypal project is set up well, and monitored. However, misunderstandings can and do arise in email communication, especially when a second language is being used between two different cultural groups, so it is well worth making your students aware of the dangers.

Conclusions | *In this chapter we have:*

- looked at the benefits of using email with learners.
- considered what basic technical and communication skills learners need to use email effectively.
- looked at how email can be used out of class.
- looked at two types of email project that can be used in class: data collection and keypal projects.
- discussed some of the issues involved in setting up and running keypal projects.

> ON THE CD-ROM YOU CAN HEAR A TEACHER TALKING ABOUT USING EMAIL WITH HER STUDENTS AND VIEW AN EXAMPLE OF A KEYPAL PROJECT.

How to use chat

- **Chat in language teaching**
- **Types of chat**
- **Chat programs**
- **Why use chat in language teaching?**

- **How to start using text or voice chat with learners**
- **How to structure a text or voice chat lesson**
- **A sample text chat lesson plan**

Chat in language teaching

Imagine a group of secondary school students in Spain text chatting to a similar group in Poland about where they live and what their town is like … or students in Argentina and in Kuwait asking each other about the customs they are most proud of in their respective countries, via voice chat. **Chat** has enormous potential to link students around the world, in real time. It is a technology that many learners will often be familiar with and will use in their social lives, so it is worth exploiting in the classroom where possible. Having said that, although the types of cultural exchange described above are hugely motivating to students, they will probably take place no more than a few times a term or semester.

In this chapter we look at the use of chat in the classroom, where the teacher can link up classes and groups in different locations, as part of collaborative project work or for one-off chat sessions such as those described above. We also look at the most likely application of chat, which is outside the classroom, where learners in the same class chat together (or with the teacher) to improve their English as part of their homework or self-study activities.

One important issue to bear in mind is that using chat needs to have a clear purpose for learners. There is not much point taking a class of learners who regularly meet face-to-face to a computer room during class time simply to chat to each other via a computer when they can do so more effectively simply by turning to their partner! We will look at ways in which chat can be effectively integrated into teaching in the next sections.

Types of chat

Chat is a tool that allows for synchronous, i.e. real-time, communication over the Internet. When talking about chat, we need to distinguish between text and audio chat, and between public and private chat, all of which can take place one-to-one or between groups of users. What makes chat essentially different from other forms of synchronous communication such as mobile phone texting, for example, is presence. Chat users are able to see the status/ availability of other chat users, such as whether the user is online, away, busy, and so on.

To start with, we'll look at some of the differences between text and audio chat, and then between public and private chat.

- **Text chat**
  Communication between chat users takes place via typed text. The user types their message into the chat program, sends it, and it instantly appears on the screen(s) of the other user(s). There is still a tendency when talking about Internet chat to assume that we are referring to text chat, but with increasing access to free voice chatware, audio chat is becoming more common.

- **Audio or voice chat**
  Communication between chat users takes place via audio, much like a phone conversation, but is conducted on the Internet. Fast gaining ground in what is known as P2P (peer-to-peer) communications software is Skype, which has the advantage of being free. We will be looking at Skype in more detail, and at other chat software, later in this chapter. For learners to use audio chat, they need to have a microphone and speakers and/or headphones.

- **Public chat**
  There are innumerable public chat rooms on the Internet, on a huge variety of topics, which any user can join. Typically, in a public chat room users do not know each other, although regular users of a specific chat room will get to know each other over time, and users may decide to use an alias instead of their real name. A typical example of a public chat forum is Yahoo! Chat (www.chat.yahoo. com), where chat rooms are grouped into categories like Business and Finance, Schools and Education, Movies, Music, and so on.

- **Private chat**
  This requires the installation of a client program, which connects individual users over the Internet. Alternatively, users may be linked over an intranet, for example within a company. Private text chat is also known as **instant messaging**. Some of the most popular instant messaging programs are Yahoo! Messenger, MSN Messenger, Google Talk, Skype and AOL Instant Messenger. Other chat programs you may come across are Qnext, .NET Messenger Service, Jabber, QQ, iChat and ICQ. Many of these instant messaging programs offer not only text chat, but voice chat, and also video and web conferencing facilities which allow the combination of video conferencing with instant messaging capabilities.

There are several different types of educational chat that one can set up with learners. One way of classifying educational chats, suggested by practising teacher Daphne Gonzalez, is set out here:

- **Free topic chats**
  Here, there is no topic or agenda set for the chat, and no specific moderator role. An example of such a chat might be learners meeting in pairs or small groups via an instant messaging program to practise English together, for example at the weekend.

- **Collaborative, task-oriented chats**
  With this, learners meet via chat out of class to complete a real task, such as preparing a PowerPoint presentation or putting together the results of a survey which they will then present to peers in the classroom. Typically, the learners

are preparing some sort of 'product' together as part of project work, and will probably have previously emailed a document or PowerPoint presentation to each other, which they can then refer to during the chat itself.

- **Informative or academic chats**
  This kind of chat disseminates information. For example, a learner or teacher gives a presentation on a topic via chat. This is then followed by a question and answer stage. Another example is where a learner or the teacher brings specific questions on a topic to be explored in the chat itself. This approach works well in the context of a blended learning solution, where learners meet some of the time online and some of the time face-to-face. We focus on blended learning solutions in Chapters 11 and 12.

- **Practice chats**
  These chats will practise a specific function or form of language, or a specific skill or strategy, and will probably take place out of class time. Examples are: a voice chat practising a telephone job interview or indeed any telephone situation; practising communication strategies such as circumlocution to describe an object; practising a specific language form such as the past tense, or future tenses for predictions; and practising pronunciation features via voice chat.

Chat programs

Let's now look at some of the chat programs currently available, for both text and voice chat. On the next page is a screenshot of Skype (www.skype.com). The Skype screenshot shows both text chat and voice chat in operation at the same time.

Most instant messaging applications include webcam (web camera) facilities, so that you can not only text chat and voice chat, but you can also see your interlocutor, if they have a webcam installed on their computer.

There are more sophisticated programs available for free, which allow video and audio conferencing alongside other tools. One well-known program is NetMeeting (http://www. microsoft.com/windows/netmeeting/), which works with Windows. If it is not already installed on your computer (for Windows 2000 and XP users), you can download it from the Internet (do a Google search of 'download NetMeeting'), and all you need to use it is a pair of headphones/speakers, a microphone and a webcam. Note, however, that with the advent of Windows Vista (2007), NetMeeting is being superseded by Windows Meeting Space. However, it is too early at the time of writing to state with any certainty whether NetMeeting will continue to be supported by Microsoft, and if so, for how long.

Meeting Space, like NetMeeting, includes both audio and video conferencing and a whiteboard facility, as well as program sharing and file transfer. Program sharing allows users to look at the same 'application' together at the same time, for example a web page, a photo or a PowerPoint presentation. File transfer allows users to send text, audio or video files to each other, from within the program. Programs like NetMeeting can be used to teach remotely, or as part of a blended learning solution. The video function will only display two users at once, so the video conferencing facility is less useful for larger groups of learners, but very well suited for one-to-one teaching or tutorials. It is also worth bearing in mind that more sophisticated types of software like this require a reliable broadband connection to work well.

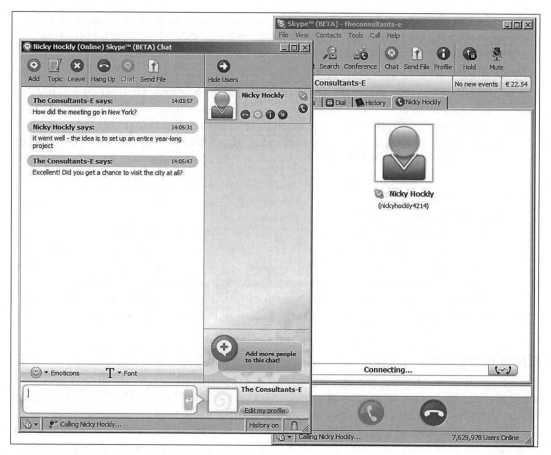

Skype in action

Why use chat in language teaching?

A teacher deciding whether to use chat with learners who meet face-to-face on a regular basis will probably want to ask the following questions:

- Does using text or voice chat with learners improve their English?
- What kind of English should learners use in chat?
- What technical skills do teachers and learners need to be able to use chat?
- What benefits does the use of chat bring to the classroom?
- Is it better to use text or voice chat with learners?

Let's consider these issues one by one.

Does using text or voice chat with learners improve their English?

There has been some research into how using tools such as synchronous text chat can improve learners' language abilities. Studies to date seem to point to text chat providing opportunities for negotiating meaning, seen as key to language acquisition by many linguists, but it has also been noted that online chat, especially text chat, does not follow the same rules of interaction as face-to-face conversation. Text chat can often appear disjointed: conversation threads get lost or questions are ignored; there are overlapping turns; and conventions for taking the floor are not automatically clear. Voice chat is more likely to make learners produce more fluent language.

What kind of English should learners use in chat?

There is the view that online text chat is the virtual equivalent to mobile phone texting, in which abbreviated forms, for example, *CU L8r* for *see you later*, are the norm. We would recommend that students generally use standard written English conventions in text chat and email. They are more likely to be interacting with other non-native speakers and writers, and abbreviated forms can be confusing. And, after all, they are meant to be using chat as another way of improving and practising their English. Perhaps worth teaching are:

- common abbreviations used in text chat, such as *btw* for *by the way*, *brb* for *be right back*, *cu* for *see you*, and so on.

- some basic rules of netiquette (or online communication etiquette), which we covered in Chapter 5. Netiquette can apply to both text and voice chat, and covers both how to behave online and some common conventions.

- in text chat, introducing learners to some basic conventions for turn-taking is worthwhile preparation for using this medium of communication efficiently and smoothly.

- example conventions include using '…' to show that you have not finished your turn and typing *?* to ask for the floor.

Below is a short extract from a teacher training chat on the use of chat, which shows how such conventions can work in practice:

MODERATOR:	OK, let's try using the chat conventions for a while – it can feel a bit restrictive, but is probably necessary …
MODERATOR:	when we try to discuss more 'meaty' topics …
MODERATOR:	such as the next one …
MODERATOR:	the pros and cons you can see for using text chat like this with your own students - over to you!
MIKE:	?
MODERATOR:	Go Mike
MIKE:	students often use it anyway, so we should be …
MIKE:	helping them with this real life skill.
JILL:	?
SUE:	?
MODERATOR:	Go Jill, then Sue
JILL:	pro - it's fun, con: takes time
SUE:	I think it's great for social activities and some language learning games, and …
SUE:	don't they know more about this skill than us …
SUE:	I mean is it a useful SKILL to teach?
MODERATOR:	Anyone?

Similarly with voice chat, as learners do not see each other, conventions are worth exploring, although the actual language used by learners, as it is in spoken form, will be closer to standard English. Even if you are able to use webcams with voice chat, it is still worth providing your learners with some guidance on turn-taking, as the video quality on webcams tends to be poor, with jerky images and sometimes a time lag between voice and image. For example, using the term *Over* or *Done* to indicate that you have finished speaking is a simple and effective way to share turns on voice chat, with or without a webcam.

Chats with more than two users will typically take place in a blended learning course, or an entirely online course. In these contexts, several learners might meet in a text chat room, or on a Skype voice conference call, with or without a teacher. In most chats with more than two users, the teacher or a learner will take on the role of moderator. The moderator introduces the chat, states the chat agenda, allocates turns in the chat, keeps participants on track, provides brief summaries of points covered in the chat and indicates when the chat is over. Below is a summary of some suggested conventions for using both text and voice chat, when there are more than two users present. You'll notice that the conventions used during a group voice chat are similar to those used for a telephone conference call.

Text chat	Voice chat
• Use *?* to ask for the floor.	• Use a convention to ask for the floor – this could be via text, or a special phrase such as *Turn please*.
• Use '...' at the end of your sentence to show that you have not finished a contribution.	• Use a special phrase or word such as *Over* or *Done* to show when you have finished speaking.
• Use '.' at the end of your sentence to show that you have finished a contribution.	• One participant should be responsible for taking notes during the chat.
• Use square brackets [ ] to make an aside to another participant, or an off-topic remark.	• The moderator can nominate quieter participants by name to contribute.
• Explain abbreviations the first time you use them in a chat, e.g. *btw = by the way*.	

What technical skills do teachers and learners need to be able to use chat?

The fact is that learners are increasingly using text and audio chat in their personal lives, as instant messaging systems become increasingly common, to communicate with family and friends, so many are already familiar with chat. Current chat software is very easy to install and use, so no special technical skills are needed by either teachers or learners, apart from knowing where and how to type comments in a chat window for text chat, and how to use a microphone and speakers, or a headset, for voice chat.

One skills area that can put learners at a disadvantage in text chat is their typing ability. Slower typists will find it more difficult to contribute, as by the time their contribution has been typed out, the conversation may have moved on. Also, if the teacher is using the text chat script for language analysis after the chat, it may be difficult to see what constitutes a mistake, and which learner errors are due to typographical errors (typos), or to the conventions of text chat.

Finally, although not a 'skill', using voice chat does require a reliable broadband Internet connection. If you have a dial-up/modem connection, it is probably safer to stick to text chat because it generally takes higher connection speeds to transmit and receive audio and video data.

What benefits does the use of chat bring to the classroom?

Using chat in the classroom – whether text or voice chat – can be hugely motivating to learners. By using chat with learners, the teacher is bringing current technology into the language learning process, creating variety by using a 'new' tool and also opening up the possibility of contacting and communicating with classes in other parts of the world. There are increasing numbers of teachers in all levels of education using chat to connect learners at a distance, from primary students to adults. We saw some real examples of this at the beginning of the chapter.

Chapter 11 provides you with suggestions of online teacher groups which you can join to link up with teachers who regularly carry out these kinds of projects in their face-to-face teaching.

Is it better to use text or voice chat with learners?

We first need to remind ourselves that text chat and voice chat are two entirely different media. Text chat requires written (typed) interaction, while voice chat relies on spoken interaction. Learners are using two different sets of skills for these two means of communication. At the same time, many chat programs combine text and voice capabilities, and some include other interactive features such as whiteboards on which to 'project' PowerPoint presentations, or to look at web pages together during a chat.

With increasingly easy access to voice chat, it is probably worth exposing your learners to a combination of both voice and text chat, if possible. As with any tool, there are a number of advantages and disadvantages associated with each, several of which have already been mentioned above, and which we summarise in the table below:

	Text chat	Voice chat
Advantages	• Learners may already use text chat at home. • Brings current technology into the classroom. • Use of a new tool can be motivating for learners. • Enables learners to make contact with learners in other countries. • A low tech option.	• Learners may already use voice chat at home. • Brings current technology into the classroom. • Use of a new tool can be motivating for learners. • Enables learners to make contact with learners in other countries. • 'Real' oral practice of language.

	• Non-threatening and easy to learn to use. • Chat transcript can be used later for language analysis.	• Voice chat software increasingly easy to download and use.
Disadvantages	• Text chat can be chaotic (overlapping turns, disjointed, topic decay ...). • Unclear whether text chat really improves learners' English. • Do we need to teach 'chat speak'? • Can be difficult to identify errors vs. typos vs. non-standard 'chat speak'. • Weaker typists are put at a disadvantage.	• Suitable for very small groups only. • Reliable broadband Internet connection needed. • Recording a chat may be complex and require other software.

How to start using text or voice chat with learners

To start using chat in the classroom, we would suggest a carefully staged approach, which will help get both learners and teachers familiar with the chat program, how it works and what it can be used for. We would suggest starting out with text chat, and then moving on to voice chat once learners have had a chance to practise with text chat. Ideally, using chat with learners would include a 'real' use of chat, for example chatting to learners in a different country, or using chat outside of class time with learners from their own class. Initially it is a good idea to use chat in class with your learners a couple of times, to help them become comfortable with it, so that they can then go on and use it outside class.

Step 1 – Install and learn to use the software

Download and install a popular instant messaging program which includes both text and voice chat facilities (e.g. Yahoo! Messenger, MSN Messenger, Google Talk or Skype – this last is especially recommended) to your school computers. If you are not familiar with instant messaging yourself, get a colleague to practise using the program with you, and make sure you understand the basics of how to use the text and voice chat in your chosen program. Note that you will need a partner to do this.

Step 2 – A practice chat class

Some of your learners may already be familiar with text or voice chat. Find out if any of your learners use chat, and if so, what for, for example to make friends on the Internet or to chat to family/friends in other countries. Also, find out how many of your learners are familiar with common instant messaging programs such as MSN, Yahoo! Messenger or Skype.

Once you have established how much chat experience and expertise you already have in the class, run a 'practice' chat session with your learners on the computer, preferably in pairs, with less experienced chat users paired with more experienced chat users. Explain clearly that the aim of the practice class is simply to encourage them to chat to each other to become familiar with the software, even if the situation is somewhat unrealistic, as learners will be sitting together in the same computer room! Make clear to learners that the goal of using chat will be for them to use chat to practise their English outside class. Remember that before learners can chat together they will need to have created a username and password for the software, and to have invited each other to join their contact lists.

First, allow your learners time to get used to using text chat, then let them experiment with voice chat, in the same chat software. This is the time to teach and practise any netiquette or turn-taking conventions that you would like your learners to use in text or voice chat. On the next page is a brief outline of a lesson for a first text chat practice session.

Step 3 – Contact with another class

The potential of chat for linking groups of learners who are far apart, in real time, is vast. How can a teacher go about setting up such a project? Through an international teachers' network (see Chapter 11) make contact with teachers who would like to link up their classes via chat, and together decide on a time to chat. It is well worth first getting the two classes to email each other to exchange some personal information, so that learners at least feel they know each other a little before chatting online. You might even want to first set up a collaborative email exchange (see Chapter 5) or a blog or wiki project (see Chapter 7), and to use chat as part of such a project.

To make the initial contact with a class in a different country less intimidating for your learners, you may first want to set up several encounters using text chat only. Once learners feel that they know each other a little, and are more comfortable not only with the medium but with chatting to each other, you could introduce a voice chat. See the following section for how chats between learners in different countries may be structured and run.

How to structure a text or voice chat lesson

Like any lesson, a chat lesson needs a clear structure and aims. First, ask yourself what learners will get out of your chat. If the chat is to be held, as we suggest, between classes in different countries, there are, as we have said, several benefits for your learners:

- contact with other learners/cultures, and the motivation that this brings.
- 'real' communication with a real purpose.
- use of a new medium in the classroom.
- a chance to practise written and/or spoken English.

There are several possible groupings for running chats between two classes in different geographical locations:

a If learners in both classes have access to individual computers, they can simply be put in pairs, with one learner from Class A being paired with one learner from Class B.

b If there are enough computers available for learners to work in small groups on a single computer, clear guidelines for turn-taking in each group need to be provided by the teacher.

c In the single computer classroom, an entire class can use one microphone for a voice chat, with the teacher allocating turns, introducing topics and signalling the various stages of the lesson.

Text chat practice session (approximately one hour)

1 Well before the class, check that the text chat program (e.g. MSN Messenger or Skype) is installed.

2 At the beginning of the class, find out if your learners are familiar with instant messaging, and if so, what they use it for.

3 Outline the aim of the practice chat session: to add each other to their chat contact lists, and to practise using text chat, so as to be able to use it outside class to practise their English.

4 Learners set up individual user accounts in the chat program, and invite each other to join their contact lists.

5 Show learners how to use the text chat feature of the program. The easiest way to do this is if you have a computer connected to a data projector, and can project the steps you take onto a screen. Otherwise, you can walk around the classroom and help learners. Ideally, each learner should use one computer alone, but learners can be paired up and take turns at chatting for the tasks below.

6 Set the learners a simple task. For example, each learner needs to chat to five other class members, and find out one unusual thing about each of these five classmates. Learners should note down what they find out, either in a word processing program or on a piece of paper. Set a time limit, e.g. ten minutes.

7 Once the time is up, stop the class. Check what they have found out about each other.

8 Repeat the activity, changing the task slightly. This time learners need to chat to five *different* classmates, to find out how many brothers and sisters they have, and their names and ages. Again, learners need to note down the information. Give a slightly longer time limit, e.g. seven to ten minutes.

9 Once the time is up, stop the class. Check what they have found out about each other. Who has the fewest/most siblings? What is the average number of siblings in the class? What is the most common name for boys and for girls?

10 (Optional) The aim of this final phase is to provide learners with more practice in using text chat, while also raising awareness of the usefulness of the tool and addressing any questions or difficulties learners may have had. If the learners have limited English proficiency, they could do this task in their first language.

Pair the learners up. If learners are already working in pairs on a computer, then pair the computers up, so that you have two computers communicating via chat. Give the learners a list of questions (for example on a prepared handout) that gets them to reflect on using chat. Suggested questions are:

- Have you used text chat before? What for?
- Do you like using text chat? Why/Why not?
- Do you think using text chat is good for practising your English? Why/Why not?
- What do you find easy about using text chat?
- What do you find difficult about using text chat?
- How could we use text chat out of class time to practise our English?
- Would you like us to use text chat during class time? Why/Why not? If yes, how often, and what for?

Give the learners time to discuss all of the questions via text chat, and then conduct open feedback with the class.

11 **Follow-up:** Announce how you plan to use text chat as part of your teaching. For example, you may want to set up an international project, based on the sample chat lesson later in this chapter, or to set learners regular text chat tasks to do with each other as homework to practise their English.

Note: If you plan to introduce voice chat to your learners, you could use a similar chat practice session, simply substituting voice chat for text chat in the steps above. Or use text chat for steps 1–9 and introduce voice chat for step 10.

For text chat, we would recommend that learners work only in grouping **a** above, as text chat can be quite slow and unwieldy, and because only one username per computer can be used easily. This makes it ideal for pairwork, where each member of the pair has access to a computer, but a lot less effective for bigger groupings. For voice chat all three groupings, **a**, **b** or **c**, can be used.

Whichever of the above groupings most suits your context, it is not a good idea to simply put two classes together via chat and leave them to get on with it. Providing a clear structure for learners to follow will give them a sense of purpose and also provide security, which is especially important if your learners are communicating in a foreign language at a distance with people who they do not know very well, and if they are unfamiliar with the chat medium. Any chat lesson, whether using text and/or voice chat, should include the following broad stages:

- **An introductory/warmer phase**
  This phase may include detailed introductions and an exchange of personal information if learners are chatting together for the first time, or it may consist of a simple exchange of information, such as 'What was the best thing you did last weekend?' for learners who have already chatted in the past. This stage serves to set the scene and acts as an icebreaker.

- **The main content of the chat**
  This may consist of one main task, or a series of short tasks, which learners need to complete, and could be based on a worksheet which learners have been given before the chat. See the sample chat lesson below.

- **A closing stage**
  In this stage learners may summarise what they have covered or achieved in the chat, and say goodbye. The teacher might have set a brief closing task, such as asking learners to tell each other one thing they have enjoyed about the chat.

A sample text chat lesson plan

This sample lesson describes a first text chat between two low language level secondary school classes who are geographically separated, preferably in different countries. The aim of the chat is for learners to find out things about their partner and to build up a profile of that partner.

Before the class

The teacher needs to first make contact with the teacher of a similar class in terms of level, class size and access to technology. As outlined earlier in this chapter, we recommend that the learners first meet each other via an email exchange, or via a class project using blogs or wikis, and that the chat allows them to meet in real time, but not for the first time. This makes the experience less threatening for learners, and provides a context for the chat encounter to take place. If learners are able to exchange digital photos of themselves before the chat, this is a good idea, too, even if this is only a photo of the entire class, but with the names of individual learners provided. Learners also need to be confident about how to use the chat program. With the teacher of the other class, set a time for the chat, divide the learners into inter-class pairs and decide on what will be covered during the chat lesson. It is also a good idea for you and the other teacher to have tried out the chat program from the computers to be used, in advance.

Classroom management issues

Ideally learners are put in pairs for the first chat, with one learner in Class A and the other in Class B, each sitting at an individual computer. For classes with fewer computers than learners, learners can either conduct the chat in pairs, or consecutive learners can be allowed access to the same computer for a certain amount of time, e.g. 10 or 15 minutes. The logistics for conducting text chat in a single computer classroom are more complex, but could involve, for example, consecutive learners or pairs of learners, each given 5 minutes to chat, and with the chat encounters spread out over several classes. On the whole, though, we would recommend using voice chat rather than text chat in the single computer classroom, as a text chat in this context is very slow and unwieldy, and those learners not directly involved in the chat will need to be kept occupied with other activities.

During the chat

First hand out worksheets, which your learners will need to complete during the chat itself. Note that each partner has a slightly different worksheet, with Worksheet A for learners in Class A and Worksheet B for learners in Class B (see opposite).

Note that these sample worksheets can easily be changed to reflect adult interests for low language level adult classes, and questions can be added (or removed), or more open questions set for higher levels. Learners text chat to their partner in the other class, and make notes on their worksheets. Writing notes and text chatting at the same time can be distracting, so an option here is to allow learners to simply chat, asking the questions on their worksheet, then ensure that their chat scripts are saved. Each learner can then print out their chat script and complete the worksheet from that, once the chat is finished.

After the chat

Each learner now has information about an individual in the other class, and can draw up a profile of that individual. This can be in the form of a written text or a grid, and ideally should include a digital photo of the learner. These profiles can then be displayed in the classroom separately or on a large poster, and digital photos of the profiles can be taken and emailed to the other class. Or the information collated could even be used to create a learner profile in an inter-class blog (see Chapter 7). Learners in Class A could be asked to decide whose profile from Class B is closest to their own: in other words, who is most like them.

A summary of issues on using text and/or voice chat with learners

- **Try the software out** in the computer room with the class before setting up the 'real' chat. This enables learners to become familiar with the chat program, with using chat itself, and for any technical limitations – such as bandwidth being too narrow to effectively use voice chat – to become apparent in advance. This is also a chance to introduce and practise any netiquette conventions and communication skills.

- When using chat between your class and a class in another country, allow them to first **make contact** with the other class, for example via a blogs project or email,

Chat Worksheet A

Ask your partner about these things, and note down the answers:

Likes and dislikes:
  favourite film
          group/singer
          colour
          pet animal
          sport
  least favourite food
           subject at school
           colour

Daily activities:
What is your partner usually doing at these times on a Sunday?
  8 a.m.
  3 p.m.
  6 p.m.
  9 p.m.

Unusual things:
Find out two unusual things about your partner.
  1
  2

Chat Worksheet B

Ask your partner about these things, and note down the answers:

Likes and dislikes:
  favourite actor
          song
          food
          subject at school
          website
  least favourite film
           sport
           colour

Daily activities:
What is your partner usually doing at these times on a Saturday?
  10 a.m.
  1 p.m.
  4 p.m.
  7 p.m.

Unusual things:
Find out two unusual things about your partner.
  1
  2

before getting them to use chat. Making contact can include exchanging basic personal information and digital photos in advance. This way learners will have fewer insecurities about talking to 'total strangers' online, a challenge even in one's native language.

- Set **a clear task**, or series of tasks, for the chat, so that learners are not left wondering what to chat about.

- Ensure that it is clear to learners what the **purpose** of using chat is. As we mentioned earlier, there is not much point using chat if the learners involved are perfectly able to talk face-to-face! Using text or voice chat with the same class all together in the computer room is fine for trying out the software and becoming familiar with chat, but the use of chat will be far more effective if it mimics real life and is used to connect people who are geographically far apart. Most effective of all is integrating chat into a wider project between classes or countries, which also uses other ICT tools such as blogs, wikis or podcasting.

- The **ideal group size** for a text or voice chat is small! The bigger the group the harder it is for participants to contribute, and for the moderator to keep things on track – and this is especially true of text chat. For us, an ideal group size is about 6 to 8 people for text chat, and 3 to 5 people for voice chat. Some chat software, such as the chat functions found in certain **Virtual Learning Environments** (**VLEs**), have break-out rooms for text chat. This means that a large group of users in a text chat can be put into smaller groups, and each group sent to a separate chat room. The moderator/teacher is then free to move between the rooms and monitor the chats.

- **Record the chat.** Most text chat programs will allow you to log (record) the text conversation as a transcript, which can then be used for analysis and/or a reminder of the content/topics covered in the chat. Some voice chat programs also allow recording, with the chat recorded as an audio file. Recording chats, whether text or voice, is useful for learners who are not able to attend a chat, as they can read or listen to the chat later in their own time. Recording chats also makes the whole experience less ephemeral, and provides a basis via the transcript or audio recording for later language analysis.

- Have **a contingency plan**! If your school's Internet connection is down, or for any reason you are prevented from being able to use the computer equipment, ensure that you have a backup plan to do something else with your learners!

Conclusions | *In this chapter we have:*

- considered how chat can be used both in and outside the classroom.
- looked at various types of chat.
- given some examples of chat programs.
- discussed why a teacher might want to use chat with learners.
- looked at some of the advantages and disadvantages of using text and voice chat with learners.
- looked in detail at how to implement text or voice chat with learners, and outlined a sample text chat class.
- provided a final summary on using text or voice chat with learners.

ON THE CD-ROM YOU CAN LISTEN TO A TEACHER TALKING ABOUT HOW SHE USES CHAT AND WATCH A TUTORIAL ON SETTING UP A SKYPE ACCOUNT.

Blogs, wikis and podcasts

- Social software
- Blogs in language teaching
- How to start using blogs with learners
- Wikis in language teaching
- How to start using a wiki with learners
- Podcasts in language teaching
- How to create learner podcasts

Social software

Blogs, wikis and podcasts are all examples of social software, computer tools which allow people to connect, to communicate and to collaborate online. A **blog** is essentially a web page with regular diary or journal entries. The term is short for *web log*. A **wiki** is a collaborative web space, consisting of a number of pages that can be edited by any user. The term comes from the Hawaiian word for 'quick'. A **podcast** is an audio and/or video file that is 'broadcast' via the Internet and can be downloaded to a computer or mobile device such as an MP3 player for listening/viewing. The word *podcast* comes from combining *iPod* and *broadcast*, iPod being the brand name for the Apple portable MP3 player. Although these three tools are different, we are grouping them together in this chapter as they have certain features in common when applied to the classroom:

- They can be set up and used by teachers and/or learners.
- They can be used to connect learners to other communities of learners, for example to a class in another country.
- The ideas and content can be generated and created by learners, either individually or collaboratively.

Although the use of ICT tools such as blogs, wikis and podcasts can be very motivating for learners, teachers are themselves sometimes fearful of the technology, or feel that they are not technically competent enough to use these tools. However, as we will see, all of these tools are easy to set up and use, with no specialist technical knowledge required.

Another common misgiving is one related to content, and the lack of control that a teacher may feel about allowing learners to generate and create their own content. Teachers may find themselves thinking: 'Will the content be appropriate? Will the language used by my learners be good enough?' In fact, these tools engender a sense of social responsibility, with learners working collaboratively on content. Also, the public nature of the content created using these Internet tools ensures that accuracy and appropriacy become more important to learners.

Blogs in language teaching

The most common type of blog is kept by one person, who will regularly post comments, thoughts, analyses, experiences of daily life, interesting links, jokes or any other form of content, to a web page. Blogs may consist of written text only, or they may include pictures or photos – photoblogs – or even audio and video.

Most blogs will allow readers to comment on blog entries, thereby creating an online community around a common topic, interest or person. We can thus see why blogs are referred to as **social software**, as they set up informal grassroots links between blogs and writers/readers of blogs. Blogs will sometimes include a **blogroll**, or list of links to other blogs which the blog writer admires, thereby widening the online community of blog writers and readers.

On the next page is a **class blog** with entries from students studying at a college in the USA. The blog was set up as part of an international exchange of infomation with students in other countries. Blogs used in education are known as **edublogs**. Edublogs cover a wide range of topics related to education, from musings on educational policy and developments to learner compositions.

An edublog can be set up and used by a teacher, by individual learners or by a class. A teacher may decide to use a blog to provide their learners with news and comments on issues, extra reading practice or homework, online links, a summary of a class for learners who were unable to attend, study tips, and so on. In this case, learners will access and read, and possibly add comments to, the blog outside the classroom. A blog set up and maintained by a teacher is known as a **tutor blog**. The teacher may decide to allow their learners to write comments in the blog. The one on page 89 (top) is an example of a tutor blog set up by a teacher in Argentina for her Cambridge First Certificate Examination preparation class. In the blog she provides study tips, reviews class work and provides extra links on specific topics such as pronunciation.

A teacher may encourage their learners to each set up and maintain their own individual blogs. These are known as **student blogs**. Learners can be asked to post to their blogs once or twice a week, or however often the teacher judges convenient, and content can range from comments on current affairs to descriptions of daily activities. Other learners, from the same class, from other classes or even from classes in other countries, can be encouraged to post comments and reactions to student blog postings. The one on page 89 (bottom) is an example of a student blog set up by a learner in Brazil. Student blogs lend themselves well to teacher training and development, too. A trainee teacher, for example, can be encouraged to reflect on what they are learning, or on classes that they are teaching, by means of a reflective blog.

The third type of blog is the class blog, one used by an entire class. Again, this blog can be used to post comments on certain topics, or on class work or on any other issue the teacher thinks interesting and relevant to learners. In a class blog learners all post to the same blog.

A class blog

A tutor blog

A student blog

Here are examples of some ways in which you can use blogs with your learners. All of these blogs could include photos, which can be taken by learners themselves, or off the Internet from free photo-sharing or clip-art sites such as Flickr (www.flickr.com).

Tutor blog	Student blog	Class blog
• Set homework.	• Personal and family information (including photos).	• Reactions to a film, article, class topic, current affairs.
• Provide a summary of class work.	• Extra writing practice on class topics.	• Things learners like/don't like doing in class.
• Provide links to extra reading/listening material.	• Regular comments on current affairs.	• A class project on any topic.
• Question and answer (e.g. about grammar, class work).	• Research and present information on a topic (e.g. an English-speaking country).	
• Exam/Study tips.	• A photoblog on learner's country, last holiday, town.	

There are some obvious advantages to using blogs in the classroom. They provide a 'real-world' tool for learners with which to practise their written English, as well as a way of contacting learners from other parts of the world if the blog is used as part of an international exchange. Even if a student or class blog is not shared with learners in other parts of the world, a blog is publicly available on the Internet. In theory anyone can read the blog, although only invited members can be given permission to add comments.

One of the issues to bear in mind when setting up student or class blogs is that of correction – how much help are learners given with their written work? Learners tend to want their written work in a blog to be as accurate as possible, given that the blog is publicly accessible, and the teacher needs to be prepared to give learners plenty of time for writing, reviewing, redrafting and checking postings before they are added to the blog. Asking learners to prepare blog entries in a word processing program, beforehand, and encouraging peer review of work in progress, for example in pairs, can help with this process.

A further area to consider is assessment. Given that a student or class blog is essentially a written assignment, blog postings can be used for evaluation. If the teacher intends to evaluate blog entries as part of a writing assessment, as with any written work the criteria for evaluation need to be made clear to learners in advance. Criteria will probably include those used to evaluate more traditional, paper-based forms of writing, such as accuracy, fluency, coherence and relevance, but they may also include criteria related to the visual nature of this electronic medium, such as the effective use of visuals, or visual presentation overall, and other areas like the length of postings and awareness of audience.

How to start using blogs with learners

A simple blogs project that you can use with learners of all levels is to get your students to set up their own student blogs, writing about themselves, their interests, family, home, country, and so on, and including some photos.

Step 1 – Setting up a sample blog (1–2 hours)

At home before class set up your own blog, including information about yourself similar to what you would like your learners to produce. Doing this has several advantages:

- It allows you to become familiar with the blog interface and how it works.

- It shows your learners what a blog is.

- It provides a model for your students' blogs in terms of: content – what the learners can write about; language – the level of language expected; and look – for example, the blog could include photos.

Step 2 – Setting up student blogs (1 hour)

Once you have shown your learners your sample blog, for which you could prepare some comprehension questions to help them understand the content, take them to your computer room, and help learners to set up their own blogs. If there are the facilities for one computer per learner, each learner can set up their own blog. If learners need to work in pairs or small groups around one computer terminal, one blog can be set up per pair/group. In the case of the single computer classroom, the teacher can set up a single blog for the entire class, with multiple users accessing it outside of class time.

Note that helping learners to set up their own blogs can be quite labour intensive! You will find yourself answering questions from learners who are all at various stages of the set-up process, so if possible it is always a good idea to put learners into pairs or small groups to set up their blogs, with one more tech-savvy learner per group to help out. Expect to spend one entire class on helping learners with the mechanics of setting up their blogs.

If you have the facilities to project a computer screen from a laptop connected to a data projector or an interactive whiteboard, you can take learners through the blog set-up process step by step on the screen, while they work on their computers.

Step 3 – Posting to and visiting blogs (1 hour)

When learners have set up their own, pair or small-group blogs, they are ready to spend some time on preparing and posting content. Once the student blogs contain several postings and photos, encourage them to share their blog addresses and to visit each other's blogs and to post comments, or in the case of a single blog with multiple posts, encourage them to comment on each other's posts in the same blog.

Step 4 – Follow-up (2–3 hours or several lessons)

Both teacher and learners will have spent some time on learning to use blogs, and on posting their initial blog entries, so it is well worth carrying on using the blogs for more than a couple of classes. Learners can be encouraged to post regularly over a certain period of time, for example, a term or a semester, with the teacher providing ideas and suggestions for content. The blogs can be kept as an internal class project, or other classes can be encouraged to visit and to comment on the blogs. Teachers can even join an international network of teachers (see Chapter 11) and get learners from other countries to visit and to comment on the student blogs. Blogs can be set so that only invited members have **commenting privileges**, which gives the blog some measure of security. This will be particularly important if you are working with younger learners.

Note that it is normal for blogs to have a limited lifespan. Only 50 percent of blogs are estimated to be active three months after being set up. Blog fatigue, or blogfade, will set in, so it is often a good idea for the teacher to have a clear time frame in mind for a blog project, such as a term or semester or a couple of months. If learners' interest doesn't flag after this time, the blogs can always be continued! You may want to experiment with using blogs for different purposes with the same classes.

How to set up a blog

There are a number of free blog sites available on the Internet. These include:

- Blogger (http://www.blogger.com)
- WordPress (http://wordpress.org)
- EzBlogWorld (http://www.ezblogworld.com/)
- Bahraich Blogs (http://www.bahraichblogs.com/)
- Getablog (http://www.getablog.net/portal3.php)

Below is the start-up page for creating your own blog in Blogger.

The blog pages freely available on the Internet tend to be very user-friendly, and setting up your own blog is usually a straightforward process, with no specialist technical knowledge or expertise needed. You simply visit the homepage of the blog and follow the instructions.

Audio and video blogs

To be able to create an audio or video blog, you need access to audio or video equipment, as well as editing software and sufficient space on a web server to store the multimedia files. Audio equipment will include a headset with microphone, and video equipment a digital video camera or webcam, although webcam images tend to be of poorer quality overall.

For audio blogging, **Audacity** is software which is easy to use (http://audacity. sourceforge.net/). Also take a look at **Audioblog** (http://www.audioblog.com/) for more details, while for video files you may want to look at **Freevlog** (http://freevlog.org/). Bear in mind that while the concept of multimedia blogs is not overly complicated, you will need some time to acquire the necessary skills, and this may also impact on your classroom time if you are planning to do this kind of project with your learners. You will need to spend a little time training them, too. If, for example, you want to try adding audio to your blogs, you will first need to teach yourself to use audio editing software such as Audacity, and then teach your students to use it, so they can record themselves. Below is an example of a video blog, or **vlog**, made by a teacher living in Japan, in which he comments on his daily life.

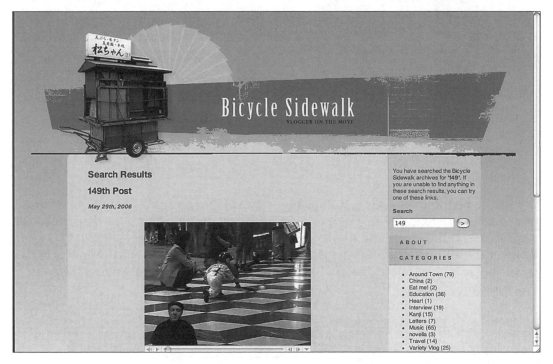

Wikis in language teaching

First of all, how is a wiki different from a blog? A blog is essentially an online journal or diary, usually written by one person, which is added to regularly. Most blogs allow visitors to add comments, which are then visible to the blog owner and also to subsequent visitors who can in turn comment further. A wiki, on the other hand, is like a public website, or public web page, started by one person, but which subsequent visitors can add to, delete or change as they wish. Instead of being a static web page or website like a blog, a wiki is more dynamic, and can have multiple authors. A wiki is like having a publicly accessible word processing document available online, which anyone can edit.

Essentially a wiki is not linear, like a blog. A blog consists of a number of postings, which are published on one web page, in reverse chronological order with the most recent posting at the top. A wiki has a non-linear structure, and pages may link back and forwards to other pages. It might be helpful to imagine the difference like this:

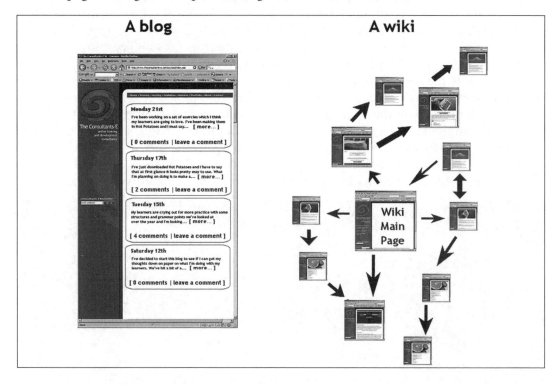

One of the best-known wikis is **Wikipedia** (www.wikipedia.org), an online encyclopedia that anyone can add to or edit. Wikipedia demonstrates several aspects of social software: it is collaborative and grassroots, displays multiple authorship and is not 'owned' by anyone. Its accuracy is a matter of debate. However, one analysis compares its overall accuracy favourably to that of Encyclopaedia Britannica. The screenshot below shows the entry in Wikipedia for the word *wiki*.

A wiki lends itself especially well to collaborative writing. The mechanics of using a wiki are relatively simple: learners can add new pages to a wiki, as well as edit previous entries/pages. One of the advantages of a wiki is that when a web page in a wiki is edited, changed or even deleted by mistake, previous versions of the page are automatically saved. This means that it is easy to see what changes have been made to pages by whom and when, and to restore an earlier version of a page. Below is the home page of a sample wiki using **pbwiki** (short for 'peanut butter wiki'), set up for a secondary school wiki project.

The screenshot above clearly shows the main functions of a wiki. At the top of the screen you can click on a tab to:

- edit the page (if you have the password).
- look at the changes that have been made by other contributors to the wiki.
- see a list of all the wiki pages.
- change the wiki settings, and add files (including pictures) to the wiki.
- log out.

At the bottom of this wiki home page are a number of links. These link to the other pages in this wiki, and have been set up in advance by the teacher. Links to wiki pages can appear within the body of text itself. They do not need to appear as a list, as in this example.

How to start using a wiki with learners

The best way to start using a wiki with a group of learners is to set up a simple collaborative writing project. A topic that we have found works well is that of '(in)famous people', in which pairs of learners write short descriptions of famous people that contain a number of humorous factual errors (but not grammatical errors!). These descriptions are then 'corrected' by another pair. The project outlined below can be used with learners of any level, and using any of the free wiki sites.

Step 1 – Preparation before lesson (approximately 30–60 minutes)

Using a free wiki site (such as pbwiki), the teacher sets up the first page of a wiki, outlining the topic of the project, and the steps the learners will need to take in the project. Below is a screenshot of the first page of the wiki set up in pbwiki. The teacher has added an image to the wiki page, and outlined the things the learners will need to do to complete the project.

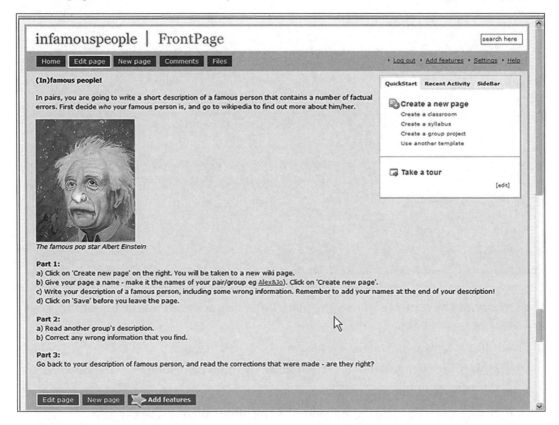

Step 2 – (In)famous people: descriptions (approximately 1 hour)

Put learners in pairs and tell them that they are going to write a description of a famous person that contains a number of factual errors. You may first want to allow them to choose and research a famous person using an online encyclopedia such as Wikipedia. They may prepare this description on paper, or in a Word document, or you could take them to the computer room, where they could type their descriptions directly into the wiki. You may want to give the learners an example of a description of a famous person with factual errors, which you have already written yourself in the wiki. The one below is an example of an erroneous entry on Albert Einstein, in the process of being written, with the wiki page in Edit mode. You will need to give the learners clear directions on how to add a new page to the wiki, and then how to add their descriptions. Once all the pairs have added their description to the wiki, let them spend time reading the other pairs' descriptions.

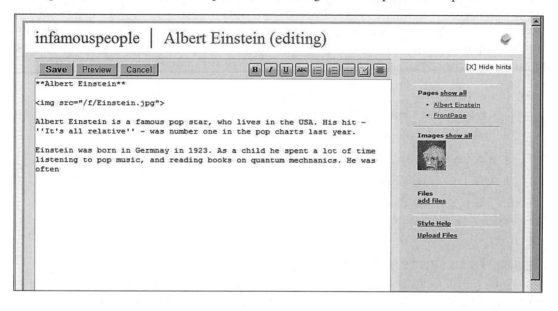

Step 3 – (In)famous people: corrections (approximately 1 hour)

Allocate one description to each pair from the previous class – make sure that it is not their own original description! The pair reads the description, clicks on the Edit tab for the wiki page and corrects any 'wrong' information in the description. Again, you may want to refer learners to an online encyclopedia such as Wikipedia for them to check any information about the famous person that they do not know. Depending on the level of the class, you could ask the pairs to now add two grammatical errors to the entry, while they are correcting the factual information. Corrections are done to the the wiki page in Edit mode. Each pair then goes back to their original description, and reads the corrections that were made. Are the descriptions now correct? If two new grammatical errors have been added, can they spot the deliberate errors and correct those, too?

Alternative (approximately 3–4 hours)

With higher-level learners a slightly more complex collaborative writing project could be set up on the same topic of famous people which uses online resources for research (see Chapter 8). In this version of the wiki project, pairs or small groups of learners each research a different facet of one famous person. For example, one famous writer, painter, musician or scientist is chosen by the class, and different aspects of their life are investigated by each pair, e.g. childhood, education, main works or influences on other artists/professionals. Each pair then prepares an entry on their topic, and creates a wiki page dedicated to this. All topics can link from the main wiki page. Groups can then read other groups' contributions and edit/change as necessary. The final result is a wiki with pages on various aspects of a famous person, rather like a mini encyclopedia.

Considerations

As with the blogs project outlined earlier in this chapter, the wiki can be kept as an internal class project, and given the public nature of the Internet, it is probably worth asking other classes/learners (for example in the same school) to take a look at the wiki, and possibly to contribute to it. In the case of younger learners, a wiki project can be viewed by parents. Knowing that the wiki will be viewed by readers outside the classroom, and will be available on the Internet for public scrutiny, is an added incentive for learners. By giving the wiki a password, only those who know the password can edit it, which gives your wiki some measure of security, but still allows it to be accessed and read on the Internet.

How to set up a wiki

There are several free sites for setting up wikis, and some of the best-known are:

- Pbwiki (www.pbwiki.com)
- MediaWiki (http://www.mediawiki.org)
- Wikihost (http://wikihost.org)

As with blogs, setting up a wiki is a straightforward process, with no specialist technical knowledge or expertise needed.

Podcasts in language teaching

The closest analogy to a podcast is that of a radio or TV show, but the difference is that you can listen to or watch a podcast on a topic that interests you whenever you want to. A podcast can be downloaded automatically to your computer using RSS, podcatching software which is described in Chapter 12. Typically, a podcast will consist of a 'show' which is released either sporadically or at regular intervals, for example every day or once a week. A podcast can be on any topic, and can include music and video. Video podcasts are also known as **Vodcasts** or **PodClips**. A podcast can last anything upwards of a few minutes to an hour or more. Podcasts can be authentic – for example, BBC radio shows are often downloadable as podcasts – or specially made for language learners.

Podcast directories are one place to start looking for podcasts. You or your learners can click on a category and scroll though a list of podcasts, listening to and subscribing to any that interest you. A podcast directory aimed specifically at teachers and learners of English is Englishcaster (http://www.englishcaster.com).

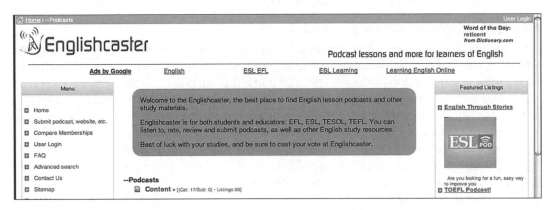

There are two main uses of podcasts in teaching. Firstly, learners can listen to podcasts made by others and, secondly, they can produce their own podcasts. It is becoming increasingly common in tertiary education, for example, for professors to record lectures as podcasts, so that students who miss a class can download the lecture podcasts for later listening on their computers or mobile devices like an MP3 player. This is sometimes referred to as **coursecasting**. Lecturers may have standard lectures that have been recorded and are made available at certain points in the university term/semester, and they may also record new podcasts regularly for their students. Podcasts can also be used in a similar way in teacher training, where trainees listen to/watch podcasts on issues of teaching methodology.

The language teacher can direct their learners to podcasts already available on the Internet, for self-study purposes, or even use them for listening in class via a computer. These can be EFL/ESL podcasts made especially for learners, such as those found at the Englishcaster directory, or authentic podcasts.

One option for the language teacher is to encourage learners to find a podcast on a topic that interests them and get them to subscribe and then listen to it regularly in their free time. EFL/ESL podcasts are available for all levels of learners, covering a wide variety of topics, from vocabulary items to discussions on topics of interest, to jokes and to learning songs. Alternatively, you can encourage high-level learners to subscribe to authentic podcasts, for example from sites such as the BBC News (http://www.bbc.co.uk).

More demanding, but ultimately perhaps more rewarding, is the option of learners actually producing their own podcasts. Learner podcasts can be a 'one-off' podcast, which is then stored on the Internet, or learners can produce a series of regular podcasts on a variety of topics, much like a radio show.

How to create learner podcasts

Learner podcasts can consist of a series of short audio files, lasting from 10–20 seconds to several minutes, made by individual learners, or of longer podcasts, made by small groups. Below are a number of ideas for podcasting projects:

Podcast idea	Suggested length of each podcast	Student language level	Individual/Small group recording	One-off/Series of podcasts
Personal information (e.g. name, age, likes & dislikes)	1–3 minutes	Low	Individual	One-off
Views on topics	1–3 minutes	Low+	Individual	Series
Describing (e.g. national customs/ holidays)	5 minutes plus	Intermediate+	Small groups	One-off/Series
Telling jokes/ anecdotes	1–3 minutes	Intermediate+	Individual	One-off/Series

Here is an example of a class podcast project.

Step 1 – Setting up a podcast page (approximately 30 minutes)

Using a free podcast site like **podOmatic** (www.podomatic.com), the teacher sets up a podcast page for the project. This needs to be done at home or in the computer room before class. To record a podcast, the teacher needs a computer and Internet connection, and a microphone and speakers or a headset. Podcast sites are extremely easy to use and no specialist technical knowledge is needed. The podcast page provides a website for learners to post their podcasts to. The teacher can provide a short text description of the project, with photos and an example podcast, as in the screenshot below, on the podcast page:

The teacher can also add a podcast as a briefing for the class, including the information that they would like learners to have in their own podcasts.

Step 2 – Creating learner podcasts (approximately 45–60 minutes)

In pairs or individually, learners prepare and rehearse a short text about themselves. Tell them to include the following information:

- name and age.
- job or school year.
- hobbies or spare time activities.
- one unusual thing about themselves.

It is important to allow learners time to rehearse their texts several times so that they feel confident about being recorded. Although their podcasts should not be directly read out word by word, do allow learners to make notes to help them, as they will feel it is important to be as accurate as possible.

A podcast site such as podOmatic will allow learners to record, listen to and then re-record their podcasts until they are entirely happy with the results. Only then should learners publish their podcasts to the podcast project page. Recording and re-recording requires no special technical knowledge or software apart from Internet access to the podcast page already set up by the teacher, and a microphone and headphones for each student to record their podcast with. The recording software is incorporated into the podcast page and is very easy to use. In the single computer classroom, learners will need to take turns to record their podcasts. When learners are happy with the recordings of their individual podcasts, they publish them to the main podcast page.

Step 3 – Listening to learner podcasts (approximately 45–60 minutes)

In a subsequent class, put learners individually (or in pairs) with a computer and allow them to listen to all of their classmates' podcasts. In the single computer classroom, the podcasts can be played one by one, via speakers. Tell learners to note down what hobbies each person has, and also the unusual thing each person mentions. Once all the podcasts have been listened to, allow learners to compare notes in small groups. What have they found out about their classmates?

Step 4 – Follow-up (3–4 subsequent lessons)

Once learners have produced one short podcast, and are familiar with the podcasting site and how to use it, they can start to produce regular podcasts on the topics which are covered in class. The more learners practise preparing podcast texts, rehearsing them and recording them, the more confident they will become, and the more 'natural' their recordings will start to sound. And the quicker they will carry them out.

Below is a screenshot of podcasts produced by EFL learners (using podOmatic) to celebrate April Fools' Day, in which the learners give original excuses for not doing their homework.

You will see that podOmatic also allows comments from listeners, which can be in text form or even recorded, if permission is given to do this. Other classes, or the parents of younger learners, can be encouraged to listen to the podcasts and to comment on them. PodOmatic is easy to use, and produces a page similar to the one on the previous page, with your podcast embedded in the page. You can choose from a variety of templates for a different look. You can also easily add photos to your audio podcasts to make the page more visually attractive.

Conclusions | *In this chapter we have:*

- introduced blogs, wikis and podcasts as examples of social software.
- looked at blogs, wikis and podcasts and how to use each of them in language teaching.
- looked at how tutor, student and class blogs can be used with learners.
- discussed how to set up simple blog, wiki and podcast projects with learners.
- introduced audio and video blogs.
- referred to software and sites to help the teacher set up blogs, wikis and podcasts.

ON THE CD-ROM YOU CAN LISTEN TO THREE TEACHERS TALKING ABOUT HOW THEY USE BLOGS AND ALSO VIEW A TUTORIAL ABOUT HOW TO SET UP A BLOG.

Online reference tools

- **Dictionaries and thesauruses**
- **Concordancers and corpuses for language analysis**
- **Translators for language analysis**
- **Encyclopedias for research and project work**

Dictionaries and thesauruses

Dictionaries

Whether your students are using bilingual, semi-bilingual or monolingual learners dictionaries in paper or electronic form, there is no denying that there is a far greater range of dictionary reference tools available than was the case even ten years ago. It is not the intention of this section to advise on the use of dictionaries in the classroom, but rather to outline some of the features that electronic dictionaries include and to show how they have developed beyond the printed page. Here we will be focusing on monolingual dictionaries. Traditionally these have been used by higher-level learners, but increasingly there is a wide range of monolingual dictionaries that have been written for students with a lower level of language proficiency.

Of course, you may well have the experience of students bringing into class small hand-held electronic dictionaries, which have translation features and audio recordings of the sounds of the words, alongside pocket-sized bilingual dictionaries in book form. The one thing we would say about these hand-held electronic dictionaries is that their content is often inaccurate and that, if you can, you should advise your students on the range of products before they purchase, as you probably have done in the past with paper dictionaries.

Virtually all of the major monolingual learners dictionaries are sold with a CD-ROM. These CD-ROMs often have some or all of these features:

- searchability (which is not alphabetically based).
- audio recordings of the words, often in both British and American English.
- games and exercises.
- information on typical errors.
- the ability to bookmark and personalise.
- thesaurus functionality.
- corpus informed information on frequency.

Some will even 'sit' in the background on your computer, allowing you to click on terms in popular word processing programs or on web pages and be taken to the appropriate dictionary entry automatically. Also, some electronic dictionaries are available free online with limited functionality, for example including the definition but not giving you the audio. Your evaluation criteria will not vary hugely from the list we looked at in Chapter 3. Suffice it to say that the more authoritative the site, the better the content will be. For dictionaries and thesauruses, try to find resources which are based on available printed materials with a good history of accuracy.

Clearly these electronic dictionaries provide a powerful resource for students working on their own and for you in the classroom. In the classroom you can have the dictionary available at all times to check the meanings of words, and, if you are fortunate enough to have a PC linked to a data projector or interactive whiteboard, you can integrate the dictionary into your day-to-day teaching seamlessly and also carry out dictionary use training sessions more effectively.

Thesauruses

While electronic dictionaries can be used at all levels, it is worth bearing in mind, initially, that thesauruses are more suited to the intermediate and advanced levels than to the elementary or pre-intermediate levels, where much more language is new to the learner. For higher levels, they can be used to enrich and extend your learners' vocabulary, whereas lower-level learners might find the variety of language on offer too overwhelming to be of any direct use.

A thesaurus can do wonders for writing projects. It can encourage learners to be more adventurous in their creative writing at the same time as helping them to analyse their output more critically. The activity below can be used as an introduction both to what thesauruses look like and to how they work.

Advanced-level thesaurus class

1 **Emotions – find the odd word out in these lists.**
   (visit http://thesaurus.reference.com and see the screenshot opposite):

disappointment	misfortune	blow	shame
happiness	blessing	elation	joy
anger	fury	rage	disgust
love	adulation	optimism	affection
envy	jealousy	resentment	relief
disgust	abhorrence	discouragement	abomination
fear	suspicion	angst	anxiety
hope	anticipation	longing	excitement
confidence	enthusiasm	assurance	resolution
regret	misgiving	contrition	caution

2 **Now find a synonym for each of the odd words out. What context are they used in?**
3 **Can you think of an antonym for each of the odd words? Use the thesaurus to help you.**

This activity, which should take less than thirty minutes, will help your learners to move around a thesaurus, and give them valuable insights into how entries are put together.

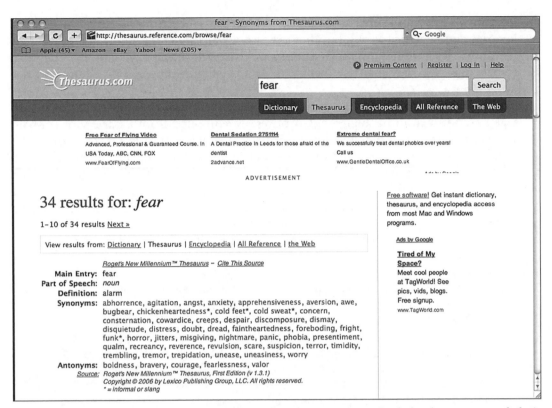

Once they have seen how the thesaurus works, have them look back at some of their writing and identify the words and phrases they tend to overuse. Encourage them to take advantage of their new thesaurus skills to research alternatives to make their writing more interesting and varied. This kind of fine-tuning of their language skills is particularly useful at examination preparation levels where an individual writing style can help them to stand out from the crowd.

Concordancers and corpuses for language analysis

A concordancer is similar to a search engine in many respects. Essentially, it is a small program that can examine large quantities of text for patterns and occurrences of particular words or phrases. Concordancers are often considered to be the domain of the language researcher or the kind of tool used by writers of grammar references and weighty linguistic tomes. And indeed they are primarily used in this domain. However, they have played an increasingly large part in the lives of materials writers in ELT over the past few years. Being able to make informed decisions on the frequency of words and structures, their collocates and particular positions in the language now influences the writing of much of the printed materials we see in our daily teaching lives, and has transformed textbooks beyond all recognition.

Projects such as COBUILD (Collins Birmingham University International Language Database), which started in 1980 under the auspices of Professor John Sinclair, have created vast **databases** of contemporary text which, in the case of COBUILD itself, led to the creation of the *Collins COBUILD English Language Dictionary*, which was based on an exhaustive study of the created database, the **corpus**. Such projects have led to better dictionaries and reference works, but they are also widely used by other writers, and their effects can be clearly seen in the coursebooks we use today, as we have said. But they also have a part to play in the classroom. Let's turn now to examine how a concordancer works, and what it does.

Concordancing involves the use of the program itself (the concordancer) and a corpus, or large body of text, to be analysed. Corpuses are compiled from a variety of sources: written collections such as newspapers or journals, or spoken collections taken from radio and television sources, or gathered on the street in audio format. The corpus of text is *tagged*, meaning that each word is described by its location, its position in relation to other words in a sentence, its frequency, and so on. The concordancer searches the corpus, asks it about a particular word and how it is used, and then you get a screen of results from a part of the corpus showing the word and enough text either side to be able to understand the context in which it is used. Here we are looking at when the words *since* and *for* occur in a corpus of spoken English.

1	He said well you've been right <u>since</u> Christmas and if you say it's
2	is. Aren't you? No I haven't been out <u>since</u> Boxing night! Wh what are you
3	secret. Obviously the law has been updated <u>since</u> eighteen ninety three. The one
4	wife and that he had been with her <u>since</u> erm she was twelve. The problem
5	You know what, I had haven't sat down <u>since</u> half past seven. What you do is,
6	how old it was. Mm So he said oh no <u>since</u> I left. I said well I, I'd still
7	And lives on there. Well I've known Derek <u>since</u> I was six weeks old. I was taken
8	pic which the EEF has been promoting hard <u>since</u> last October. We've been doing
9	Act which, and we've had that law <u>since</u> nineteen sixty eight. So we've
10	asking. I'm, I'm asking, I've been here <u>since</u> Saturday now I've sat here
1	bits in there for her a few kittens in there <u>for</u> a couple of days I, so they'd
2	they're married and they've been married <u>for</u> a couple of years I reckon,
3	going, you should of said oh I just come up <u>for</u> a few days. Blair had to look
4	your toes. We've still got that tape <u>for</u> a couple of a weeks. Haven't
5	we do, but when he goes back to work now <u>for</u> a couple of days it'll take
6	of February er so. So he was only in <u>for</u> a couple of days then?
7	mate! Are you cheeky! Had a sore throat <u>for</u> a couple of days! Hiya
8	yeah that way. It won't be like it <u>for</u> a couple of years. But he's
9	who's friend of Mat's? That's right yeah, <u>for</u> a little bit, I was on about
10	that'll say ah yeah we've been doing this <u>for</u> a little while, why don't we

As you can see from these simple examples, it is quite possible to extrapolate basic rules about the way *for* and *since* work. This is a simple example of the power of concordancers – and one which certainly could be used with lower-intermediate levels, if the right output was chosen.

When working with concordancing we have the option to download and install both a concordancing program and a variety of corpuses (often called *corpora* in the formal or technical literature) to our own computers, or use an existing website which queries corpuses online. It is often the case that concordancing programs will be commercial, and websites will not. In this section we will list some of the main concordancing programs and corpuses, but will concentrate on free online resources for getting started in this area.

Concordancing programs

- Monoconc (www.monoconc.com), $69.

- Concordance (www.concordancesoftware.co.uk), $99.

- Paraconc [for parallel corpuses] (www.athel.com), $95.

- Wordsmith Tools (http://www.lexically.net/wordsmith/index.html), $92.

(All prices at the time of writing.) Note that most of these programs will come with some corpuses – or text collections – already included to get you started. The ICAME Corpus Collection CD-ROM, for example, includes a set of corpuses and a copy of Wordsmith Tools (for more information, visit the site at: http://helmer.hit.uib.no/icame/newcd.htm).

Corpuses

When choosing a concordancer, the main evaluation criterion, apart from the price and ease of use of the software, will be the type of language you want to work with: spoken or written, American or British English, legal or journalistic, and so on. These choices will influence which corpus you decide to query, and what kind of results you will get. These are some of the most well-known corpuses. Please note that access is usually through subscription.

- British National Corpus (http://www.natcorp.ox.ac.uk/), 100 million words.

- COBUILD (http://www.collins.co.uk/books.aspx?group=155), 56 million words.

- International Corpus of English (http://www.ucl.ac.uk/english-usage/projects/ice-gb/index.htm),1 million words.

- American National Corpus (http://americannationalcorpus.org/), 22 million words.

For a more complete guide to available corpuses go to David Lee's City University of Hong Kong collection at http://devoted.to/corpora. This page includes corpuses which can be accessed freely online or downloaded and incorporated into a concordancer program.

For those who do not want to spend money there are web-based alternatives which are both free and extremely useful and, while they might not help a writer of grammar books or ELT reference materials, are certainly good enough for classroom use. One such resource is the LexTutor online concordancer designed by Chris Greaves at the Polytechnic University of Hong Kong (you can find the site at: http://www.lextutor.ca/concordancers/concord_e.html).

At first, the page may seem daunting, and indeed there are plenty of options to tinker with, but for a simple concordance, put the word you want to find out about in the text entry box marked 'Keyword', choose the corpus you would like to search from the drop-down 'In corpus' list and then hit the 'Get concordance' button. You will see results similar to the *for* and *since* examples above. The corpuses on this site are generally limited samples of some of the bigger ones available. They include:

- 1,007,000 words of the written British National Corpus.

- 965,000 words of the spoken British National Corpus.

- 1,000,000 words of the Brown Corpus of Standard American English.

There is also a variety of other, smaller corpuses totalling over four million words. It is possible to search one corpus, or all at the same time. You should not feel that you necessarily need access to the larger corpuses to use concordancers effectively. Chris Tribble, who has a regular column in the Guardian Weekly ELT section devoted to the subject, has argued that much smaller corpuses can be of equal use (http://www.ctribble.co.uk/text/Palc.htm).

Use in class

But what is the use of all this data in the classroom – and is it only useful for higher levels? The answer to the second part of that question, as we saw above with the concordances on *for* and *since*, is definitely not! Those examples could certainly be used with lower levels to initiate some thought and discussion on the use of these two words. The answer to the first part of the question is slightly longer.

You can use the corpus for generating test material such as cloze exercises and exam practice materials. At higher levels, a corpus can serve as a useful reference tool in the classroom for the more intricate examples of language use. For example, 'What's the difference between *glisten* and *glitter*?' Parallel concordancers, which compare texts in two or more languages, can also be useful for examining how structures are dealt with in first and second languages. Let's turn to an example class now, using *go to* (+ *the*) on the opposite page. Notice that for this concordance we have chosen to sort right, ensuring that the words following the search results are in alphabetical order. This makes it easier to see which words occur with *go to the* and *go to*, and in what frequency. A concordancer will also allow you to sort left, ordering words prior to the search term.

For another useful discovery activity, try blanking out the target words in concordances and having your learners work out which word is missing in each. Although this sounds quite easy, it can turn out to be more difficult than you think and is only suitable for higher-level language learners. Make sure that the examples you use are logical enough for your learners to be able to find the missing word. Try this one as an example:

1	York greenbelt to protect Skelton. It is,	xxxxxx,	a function of Skelton to
2	Mhm and erm in erm, speaking about it	xxxxxx	and in mentioning about the
3	were a mythical thing. Xxxxxx,		as we write these continuous
4	Northern Region support a Special Report. Xxxxxx,		at our pre-congress meeting,
5	on the way to improved working conditions. Xxxxxx,		before these aims can be
6	want to get through the business we can and	xxxxxx	busy we are, erm. I wouldn't
7	be doing that quite quickly. Can I start,	xxxxxx,	by telling you what this case
8	the problems that might arise erm there is,	xxxxxx,	cause for some er optimism
9	they won't be inheriting anything anyway	xxxxxx	close they may be. And the
10	know I reckon er when it is... Yeah,	xxxxxx	did they employ him? He's had

1 **Which word is missing from the sentences above?**
2 **How did you work out the missing word (think about location, punctuation, etc)?**
3 **What conclusions can you draw about the use of the word?**
4 **What is the difference in use of the word in examples 6 and 9, and in example 10?**

Key: The missing word is *however*. It often starts a sentence, and is immediately followed by a comma. When it is in the middle of a sentence it is often preceded and followed by a comma, marking a pause. It often introduces a counterpoint. In sentences 6 and 9 it conveys the meaning of 'no matter how'. In example 10 it could be replaced by *Why*.

Sample concordancer class (lower level)

1 **Look at these example sentences. Which ones are correct?**
   - I must go to the bank and get some money out.
   - I go to the school every day at 9 o'clock.
   - Do you fancy going to the cinema?
   - Let's go to the office and get some work done.
   - Our son goes to the local secondary school.
   - You need to go to hairdresser's.
   - Could you go to the supermarket and get some milk?
   - Do you go to the bed early?

   Can you correct the incorrect ones?

2 **Check your answers with a partner. Now look at the sentences again. Is there a rule for when we use *go to* and when we use *go to the*?**

3 **Now look at these real examples from LexTutor. Do these examples fit your 'rule'?**

to the firm at Oxon and er I had to	go to the	bank and borrow the money,
and so, I had to go to, I had to	go to the	bathroom to the toilet very,
the idea that you weren't going to	go to the	county school? She was very
with that on. So don't	go to the	hairdressers before us,
for the next lesson, I could	go to the	library and I used to sit
in the market. You	go to the	market, and I've been to the
MacDonalds and then we could	go to the	museum as well, that's free
Yeah. But re r Bren wanted to	go to the	pub. Well I don't, I, I
Well yes you could	go to	antique shops and buy that
to sleep. We wake up and well we	go to	bed about half past ten,
Put on the clothes you put on to	go to	church on Sunday. You must
two police officers are to	go to	jail for their part in the
into Scotland. He did not even	go to	London much, but lived in
I couldn't get up! On Monday to	go to	school. I could not get up!
ten percent of children	go to	special schools e.g. The Petö
No. I'd be quite happy to	go to	work if erm if I had a good

4 **Now get together with another pair and make a list of when we use *go to* and when we use *go to the*:**

   go to   **go to the**
   bed

   Can you add any more examples?

5 **Compare your list with the rest of the class.**

While they can certainly be useful, concordancers can also bring a lot of 'noise' into your classroom in the form of language that may be unfamiliar to your learners and which may be distracting for them, so distracting in fact that they detract from the main aims of your lesson.

A tool like this, which gives access to such a quantity and richness of language, should be used sparingly and thoughtfully, when you think that the discovery approach may lead to a better understanding of the language you are dealing with at that moment. You may also find that it is better to tailor the results of a concordance and present it in the form of a word processed document, rather than give access to the concordancer itself to your learners. A concordancer can be a powerful ally and helper, even in the single computer classroom, and is another tool to add to your collection of useful applications.

Whatever approach you adopt, make sure that the corpus fits what you are teaching, test the concordance results beforehand so that you are not caught unawares by the results your learners may get, and ensure that they are comfortable with the tool and the technology, leaving them free to concentrate on what it produces, rather than the production process itself. For more freely-available web-based concordancers, try the following sites:

- British National Corpus (http://www.natcorp.ox.ac.uk/), limit of 50 results.
- Bank of English (http://www.collins.co.uk/Corpus/CorpusSearch.aspx), limit of 40 results.

Translators for language analysis

Translation software is still in its infancy and at the time of writing remains unreliable and in many instances of dubious quality. However, it is worth mentioning, if only to point out to your learners the dangers it poses if they use it inappropriately, for example to carry out a translation assignment into their own language. The AltaVista site, Babel Fish (http://babelfish.altavista.com/), leads the way in offering quick web-based translation, but you shouldn't expect great results from anything other than single words or very simple phrases. Nothing you will find on the web will be able to cope with the famous Groucho Marx one-liner, *Time flies like an arrow. Fruit flies like a banana.*

By now you may be asking yourself why we are discussing translation sites at all. The simple answer to that is that it is precisely their fallibility and simplicity that make them interesting vehicles for getting learners to notice the language they are working with, to recognise structures and to process language in an engaging and often amusing way.

An intermediate translation class

Apart from being a fun activity, this involves quite a lot of language processing, and also highlights the problems of relying too heavily on technology.

While the translation back into English opposite isn't perfect, Babel Fish Translator was never intended to go backwards and forwards between languages like this. The original translation into Spanish was good enough to be understood, and we have used the site a few times to get an idea of the content of certain web pages in languages we do not speak, or even to engage in text chat with speakers of other languages.

This text was translated from the original English into Spanish by the Babel Fish translator at AltaVista. The Spanish version was then translated back into English. As you can see, it wasn't a perfect translation. Work with a partner and try to construct the original text.

Translation back into English

Hi! My name Gerard Hunt and I am English professor and technologist. Alive and work in Caracas, Venezuela, and I have here been by 17 years. Work with two colleagues, and we specialized in line in the education. Caracas is a great place and really joy living here. There is abundance to do – the museums, the stores, the cinemas and the galleries of art and the food and the wine are great!

Original text

Hi! My name is Gerard Hunt and I am an English teacher and technologist. I live and work in Caracas, Venezuela, and I've been here for 17 years. I work with two colleagues, and we specialise in online education. Caracas is a great place and I really enjoy living here. There's plenty to do – museums, shops, cinemas and art galleries and the food and wine are great!

Encyclopedias for research and project work

It used to be the case that having access to an encyclopedia meant also needing to have a large set of shelves on which to store all of the volumes. This collection of volumes then became a small CD-ROM sitting next to our computers, and these days is more likely to be a collection of web addresses to useful and authoritative sources online. Informational reference sites based on printed material are a good starting point and here we would include paper-based volumes such as the Encyclopedia Britannica, as well as Microsoft Encarta, which was originally published on CD-ROM.

Do check out how often the content is updated. Microsoft Encarta is updated regularly, but more regularly for premium subscribers than for the free version. Wikipedia is updated every minute of every day, but then we have to bear in mind that it has thousands of editors worldwide, with varying degrees of experience. All this must be weighed up when deciding which to use. In the end referencing a variety of sources may help. Sites such as Encyclopedia Britannica, Encarta and the Columbia Encyclopedia can safely be considered both accurate and fairly comprehensive, but with some this may not be the case. It is worth remembering the caveat made in Chapter 7 about Wikipedia being user-produced, and therefore potentially prone to inaccuracies.

The wealth of information contained on these sites opens up the world to our learners in a way that more traditional collections of classroom objects simply can't. Project work, biographies and other fact-based lessons become less arduous for our learners, leaving them free to concentrate on the language side of things, and able to access the information they need for any particular task from a reliable source. On the next page is an example of a fact-finding activity which involves lower-level learners using encylopedias to find out information about a country they are interested in.

1 What do you know about your chosen country? Complete this chart.

	What I know
Name	
Capital city	
Autonomous communities	
Population	
Average age	
Languages	
National holidays	
Flag	

2 Visit three encyclopedia websites and complete your chart.

	britannica.com	wikipedia.org	encyclopedia.com
Name			
Capital city			
Autonomous communities			
Population			
Average age			
Languages			
National holidays			
Flag			

3 Compare your country with others in your group. What are the big differences?

Note: In a monolingual class this part of the activity can be a group knowledge-building exercise with everyone exchanging what they know to build up a bigger picture.

4 Now write a short report on your country. Include some pictures from Google.

Note: Entries may vary from encyclopedia to encyclopedia, depending on the depth of each article, and when each one was updated. It would be useful to discuss this with your group.

Conclusions | *In this chapter we have:*

- considered the use of online dictionaries, thesauruses and translation services.
- examined the role of concordancers and corpuses in lesson planning and teaching.
- examined the use of online encyclopedias, and considered how they provide access to a much-needed 'world knowledge' in the classroom.

> ON THE CD-ROM YOU CAN LISTEN TO A TEACHER TALKING ABOUT USING ONLINE REFERENCE TOOLS AND GO ON A TOUR OF A LONGMAN DICTIONARY.

Technology-based courseware

- **CD-ROMs and DVDs**
- **Evaluating CD-ROMs**
- **Computer-based testing**
- **Electronic portfolios**
- **Interactive whiteboards**

CD-ROMs and DVDs

CD-ROMs

First of all, what exactly is a CD-ROM? Short for 'Compact Disc Read-Only Memory', a CD-ROM looks exactly like an audio CD but contains multimedia files that are programmed to use text, images, audio and video to provide interactivity. CD-ROMs are often included free or at little extra cost with coursebooks and workbooks. CD-ROMs accompanying courses typically have content related to each course unit, providing learners with extra reading and listening materials, recording functionality to practise pronunciation and speaking, and with grammar and vocabulary activities like matching vocabulary to definitions, drag and drop exercises, gap-fills, crosswords, and so on.

These CD-ROMs are primarily designed for learners to work on alone as follow-up to a lesson, either in a school self-access centre or at home. They can include features such as allowing learners to choose their own path through the CD-ROM materials by making their own 'lesson plans' – choosing which activities to do and in what order to do them. Many coursebook CD-ROMs also have testing materials incorporated, so that learners can check their own progress, as well as a grammar reference section and mini-dictionary. As well as the CD-ROMs accompanying language coursebooks, there are standalone CD-ROMs aimed at different groups of learners which cover different language areas and skills, such as examination preparation and practice, grammar and vocabulary and pronunciation. And of course there are dictionary CD-ROMs, which we covered in Chapter 8.

Pronunciation practice usually involves a learner listening to a word or short sentence, and then recording themselves while repeating the word or sentence. The learner's output is then compared to a 'model' of correct pronunciation and the results displayed to the learner, often in the form of a graph. What is known as **voice recognition software** is used for this type of pronunciation activity. Note that voice recognition software is not always reliable, and even native speakers can be given negative feedback if their accents do not match the model provided!

CD-ROMs are particularly strong on providing grammar practice activities, and listening and reading materials for learners. CD-ROMs are less effective for speaking practice, as it is difficult to move beyond a 'listen and repeat' model, given the technology currently available and the lack of 'real' interaction inherent in a CD-ROM. Writing, too, will tend to be limited to 'fill in the blanks' activities, or reordering sentences into paragraphs or comparing paragraphs to a model. Any longer texts or creative writing produced by the learner will need to be corrected by the teacher, which makes practice of the writing skill less suited to this kind of self-study.

DVDs

Starting to make an appearance along with CD-ROMs in the language teaching world are DVDs – short for 'Digital Versatile Disc' – which were developed in the 1990s. These are similar to CD-ROMs in that a variety of data can be stored on them, but they have much greater **storage capacity** than CD-ROMs. DVDs are usually used as an alternative to video cassettes, which are becoming increasingly outdated. DVDs allow the viewer to choose from various language options. On an EFL coursebook DVD you will generally find more video, which takes up a lot of disc space, than you would find on a CD-ROM. The video content on a DVD can be viewed on a computer with DVD viewing software installed, or on a DVD player. Note, though, that DVDs featuring interactive exercises need a computer. Some people believe that DVDs will eventually replace CD-ROMs in the EFL world, given their superior storage capacity and the high quality of video and audio. One particularly useful feature of DVDs is that there is often an option to view subtitles along with a video dialogue. In ELT courseware DVDs these subtitles are generally only in English, but in authentic DVDs, such as feature films, they can be in a choice of several languages. There are several ways the subtitles in DVDs can be used with learners in an English class. Here are a few ideas:

- The subtitles for a dialogue are hidden during a first (and even second) viewing. How much the learners understood can then be checked with comprehension questions, and the dialogue played a final time with the subtitles displayed.

- Learners listen to short sections of a DVD dialogue several times, transcribe them and then check their version of the transcript with the subtitles.

- Learners watch a short DVD dialogue between two characters with the audio switched off, reading the subtitles several times. Pairs are then invited to each take a character role, and to read the subtitles for their character at the same time the dialogue is played again, still with the audio switched off. This can be repeated several times. Can the learners keep up with the lip movements of their characters? Finally, the dialogue is played with the audio switched on.

While the use of DVDs of feature films is not a feature of using technology-based courseware, it is worth pointing out that you can exploit the use of native language subtitles for English language films, if you teach in a monolingual context. Play a short dialogue from an English language film, with the sound switched off, and only the native language subtitles displayed. Allow learners time to translate their native language into what they think the characters are saying in English. Replay the sequence several times with the sound still off, so that learners can check their translations with the lip movements of the characters on the DVD. Finally, play the sequence again with the sound on. Compare and discuss any differences in the translations.

Using CD-ROMs with learners in the classroom

Given that CD-ROMS are readily available and easy for learners to use, one of the first issues to resolve is whether to encourage your learners to use them entirely alone at home or in the self-access centre, or whether to integrate them into the classroom in some way. Self-study use of CD-ROMs at home is only possible, of course, if learners each have their own copy of a CD-ROM (or if the self-access centre in a school allows learners to take CD-ROMs home) and access to a computer. There are several types of activities that can be done to integrate a CD-ROM into your lessons:

- In the single computer classroom or school, pairs of learners can take turns to do a few CD-ROM activities, for example a couple of grammar drag-and-drop activities, while the rest of the class are busy with paper-based activities on the same grammar point. This introduces variety into the classroom.

- If you have access to a data projector (or 'beamer') and one computer, CD-ROM or DVD content can be projected onto a screen for the whole class to view and work on together, with learners taking turns to take control of the computer mouse. This is especially useful with video content, which in itself adds variety to the lesson. Using a data projector is also an excellent way to train your learners about what is on the course CD-ROM and how they should use it at home or in the self-study centre.

- If the school has a computer room or self-access centre, the teacher can programme in regular short sessions, for example once a week or fortnight, in which learners work alone or in pairs on CD-ROM materials during class time. Note that these sessions should be kept short so that learners don't get bored or lose focus.

Evaluating CD-ROMs

CD-ROMs are often cited as being particularly motivating for learners, as they use 'new' technology, provide a multi-sensory alternative to paper-based classroom work, encourage self-study and autonomous learning, and can expose learners to authentic language via audio and video. The truth of the matter is that, like any tool, overuse can undermine the 'novelty' effect for students. Also, CD-ROMS have now been around since the late 1980s, and are being increasingly superseded by newer technologies such as blogs, podcasts, instant messaging, and so on, which we have already discussed in earlier chapters. The one big advantage that CD-ROMs have over these newer Internet-based technologies is that learners can work with CD-ROMs offline, and are thus not reliant on an Internet connection, which in some contexts may be unreliable, expensive or simply not an option.

Given the wealth of CD-ROMs available for learners of English, where do you, the teacher, start in terms of evaluating whether one CD-ROM or another will be 'better' for your learners? In reality, teachers usually make the pragmatic decision of encouraging their learners to work with the coursebook CD-ROM (if there is one) in their own time, or refer them to the self-access centre. However, for those teachers who need to either recommend CD-ROMs to their learners, or are asked to choose CD-ROMs for their resource centres, where do you start?

The first issue to consider is whether a specific CD-ROM is meant to be a standalone resource, for example a CD-ROM for exam practice, or if it is an additional resource for a course. We will now consider how to evaluate a freestanding or standalone CD-ROM. Asking the following questions, and matching them to the needs and interests of your learners, will help in this process.

- What age group is the CD-ROM aimed at? Is the content suitable for adults, adolescents or younger learners? Is the content suitable for the cultural context in which you teach?

- What linguistic level is the content aimed at – beginners, elementary, intermediate or advanced?

- What kind of English is being focused on, for example business English, general English, English for academic purposes, and so on?

- How 'interesting' are the materials, and how well are they presented? Is the CD-ROM easy to navigate around? Is there a range of activity types and is enough variety provided?

- What skills and language areas are focused on – reading, writing, listening, pronunciation, vocabulary or grammar?

- Is it clear to the learners what the aim of individual activities is?

- How much multimedia content, especially video and audio, is there? What is the quality like? How much authentic audio/video is there, and how suitable is this for your learners?

- How is feedback on activities given to learners? Does feedback, although automated, help students really learn from their mistakes, and if so, how?

- How is testing integrated into the CD-ROM, and how do learners measure their own progress through the materials?

- What additional resources are provided, for example a dictionary or glossary, grammar paradigms and explanations?

- Are non-linguistic areas, such as intercultural communication skills, learner training or differences in learning styles, addressed in some way? If so, how?

- Does the CD-ROM meet any accessibility laws you may face?

Finally, you might want to consider what using a CD-ROM really adds to your learners' language learning experience, and how motivated they will be to use CD-ROMs, before you invest in CD-ROM resources. One way to do this is to discuss their value with your learners directly. It is also important to provide both teachers and learners with hands-on training in the use of CD-ROMs, and to link classroom work as far as possible with self-study CD-ROM work. Encouraging learners to keep a learning log of their self-access work and achievements, and even integrating this activity into your method of assessment, are ways of ensuring a sense of continuity between classroom work and self-study CD-ROM work.

Computer-based testing

Computer-based testing, online testing, e-assessment ... all of these terms refer to a phenomenon which has become increasingly visible in English language teaching in the last few years, that of taking tests via a computer rather than on paper. EFL learners can now take a range of different tests and examinations via a computer. Here are some examples:

- Learners can be given a diagnostic test on a computer before they start a course. This assesses their language levels in the skills of reading, writing, listening and even in discrete-item pronunciation, as well as in grammar and vocabulary. This information can then be used to assign the learner to a certain class or language programme, although for more thorough diagnostic testing, most institutions will also include a spoken interview and ask for a sample of the learner's writing.

  One commercial diagnostic text is the Quick Placement Test (QPT), which is available both on CD-ROM and in a pen-and-paper version. Learners answer multiple-choice questions which test their listening, reading and grammar skills. The learner's test results are presented against the ALTE (Association of Language Testers in Europe) Framework and the CEF (Common European Framework).

Test result

You have now finished the test.
The QPT estimates your ability at ALTE Level 3: Upper Intermediate

ALTE Level	Council of Europe Level description	Council of Europe Level	Cambridge Examinations
5	Mastery (Very Advanced)	C2	CPE
4	Effective Proficiency (Advanced)	C1	CAE BEC Higher CELS Higher
3	Vantage (Upper Intermediate)	B2	FCE BEC Vantage CELS Vantage
2	Threshold (Lower Intermediate)	B1	PET BEC Preliminary CELS Preliminary
1	Waystage (Elementary)	A2	KET
0.5	Breakthrough (Beginner)	A1	
0			

This result should not be used as an absolute indication of your ability, but should be viewed in conjunction with other forms of assessment.

You may wish to discuss this with your teachers.

quick placement test

Exit from sample test

The results screen showing the student at ALTE Level 3: Upper Intermediate

The QPT is commercially available from Oxford University Press, but there are also diagnostic test resources freely available online. Below is an example of an online diagnostic level test for a private English language school.

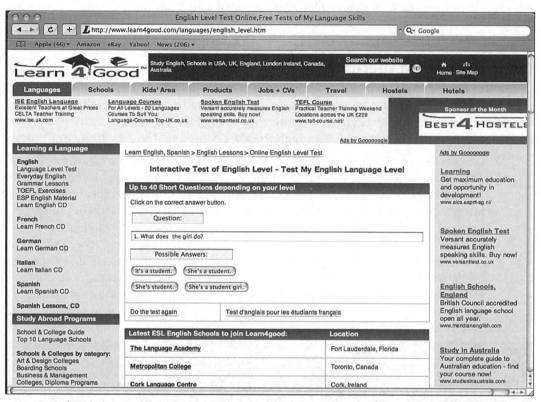

What is important to note is that both of these tests are examples of adaptive tests. The computer offers a question, and depending on the learner's answer, it mathematically estimates the level of ability and then finds a second question that matches that level of ability. It does the same with the next question, the second time revising its estimation of the learner's ability based on the two answers it now has. The same process continues with each question, and each time the computer has more information on which to base its estimate of ability, which becomes increasingly accurate as more questions are asked.

Note that the free language school adaptive diagnostic test above is based purely on the recognition of grammar items. More sophisticated commercially available diagnostic tests (either online or via CD-ROM) will take into account a range of skills, and will recommend learning strategies for individuals based on their test performance, as well as point learners to their equivalent test scores in recognised examinations or tests like TOEFL or TOEIC.

- Learners can take simple progress tests on CD-ROM. These tests will be based on the work that the learners have been doing in their coursebooks. Tests are often included in the learner's coursebook CD-ROM, or 'Test Master' CD-ROMs are made available for teachers as editable Word files. Teachers can then use ready-made tests, or make new tests for their learners, based on coursebook material.

Some publishers are starting to produce programs, or banks of online materials (often linked to courses), that enable teachers to create their own digital tests at the touch of a button.

- Learners can take internationally recognised examinations on a computer, for example the Internet-based TOEFL Test from ETS.

Advantages and disadvantages of computer-based testing

For the large international examination boards there are obviously several important advantages in being able to offer examinations online. By offering increased flexibility in location (learners can take an exam in many more centres geographically online) and in timing (an exam can be offered more frequently online), their market is considerably expanded and convenience to the customer improved. With computer-based testing, the mechanics of marking and feedback can be automated to a much greater extent, and results provided to candidates more quickly than with a paper-based exam. Marking of certain items is also much more reliable by computer than by hand, although examining speaking and writing skills still requires human intervention. The long-term costs of developing and running online exams are also considerably lower than those for face-to-face examining.

The main disadvantage of computer-based testing in our field continues to be that of ensuring reliability in the marking of extended pieces of writing and in assessing speaking. In this sense, nothing has changed from paper-based testing, as examiners are still needed and inter-rater reliability is difficult to guarantee. One other disadvantage is that initial investment costs in computer-based testing tend to be high, as software especially designed for specific computer-based tests is developed and an item bank of 'questions' and resources is built up.

A further important issue is that of authentication with distance testing: how does the examiner know that the person taking the test online is indeed who they claim to be? With the advent of optical and fingerprint recognition technology, we may start to see more official examinations and tests delivered online, with students taking them from home, but at the time of writing this is still an area in development. Security is an ongoing issue for anyone involved in setting examinations.

For the language teacher, the main experience of computer-based testing is likely to be that of using computer-based progress tests or in preparing learners to take one of the internationally recognised exams online – and again, there are several CD-ROMs on the market that provide learners with exam practice that mimics the real thing (see page 120).

Electronic portfolios

Related to the area of online and computer-based assessment, are electronic portfolios, also called **ePortfolios** or **digital portfolios**. A traditional paper-based portfolio is a collection of a learner's work, and an ePortfolio simply means that this work is presented in electronic format, and can thus include various electronic media such as video, audio, blogs or websites, as well as documents. An ePortfolio can showcase a range of the owner's skills, and display achievements not just from formal learning situations, but also from extra-curricular activities or work experience. The portfolio may also include reflections on the learning experience itself.

Name: Adrian

Time left **88 mins**

Read the text and choose the correct word for each space. First, click on the gap and a choice of words will appear. Then, select the correct answer **A, B, C** or **D**.

Test 1: Reading Part 5: Question 26

PEARSON
Longman

◄ **26** 27 28 29 30 31 32 33 34 35 ►

Modigliani - an Italian artist

Nowadays cards and posters of pictures by Amedeo Modigliani are popular with people all [26] the world, but the artist himself did not have an easy life. He [27] born in Livorno, Italy, in 1884. His father was a businessman who did not make [28] money, and his mother [29] a school.

Modigliani went to art school in Florence and Venice, before moving to Paris [30] he painted and made sculptures. His work was [31] by art from Africa which he saw in museums. He was very poor and not very strong, and after a [32] years he gave up making sculptures. He painted people in a gentle, thoughtful style.

Many of his most beautiful paintings [33] Jeanne, the woman he loved. Often the people in his paintings look sad or tired. Perhaps Modigliani was painting his own feelings. [34] in the end he began to [35] a little money, he was never very successful in his lifetime.

26

A ○ over

B ○ on

C ○ through

D ○ along

Part 1: | Part 2: | Part 3: | Part 4: | Part 5:

READING 1 2 3 4 5   6 7 8 9 10   11 12 13 14 15 16 17 18 19 20   21 22 23 24 25   **26** 27 28 29 30 31 32 33 34 35

Part 1: | Part 2: | Part 3:

WRITING 1 2 3 4 5   6   7

FINISH TEST   QUIT

From the Longman PET (Cambridge Preliminary English Test) Practice Test CD-ROM

A portfolio is considered to be a richer way of assessing students, as it provides a much clearer idea of learner achievements and products than test scores or grades. ePortfolios are becomingly increasingly common in education, especially in secondary schools and further education institutions, reflecting the growing importance of, and access to, technology in our lives, as well as the rise of the electronic job market. A learner applying for a job with a company can send an ePortfolio of work to a prospective employer easily and quickly, and so display a range of skills not reflected in a test score.

Portfolio building is generally an ongoing process, and may include materials from courses already taken by learners, as well as current projects and works in progress. Opposite (top) is a diagram of areas that might be included in an ePortfolio. This is a comprehensive overview of what could be included in an ePortfolio. Learners and teachers can choose from all of these elements and include what seems most relevant to the learner's needs and interests, and to the aims of the portfolio. The content of an ePortfolio belonging to an adult learner of business English working for a multinational company will obviously be considerably different from that of a secondary school learner whose ePortfolio is part of their overall English class annual assessment. Opposite (bottom) you can see an example of the opening page of an Italian student's ePortfolio. Susana has put links to her work in the right- and left-hand columns of the ePortfolio main page.

There are several open source (free) software packages which learners can use to create an ePortfolio. One of these is Elgg (http://elgg.org/), a platform that allows documents

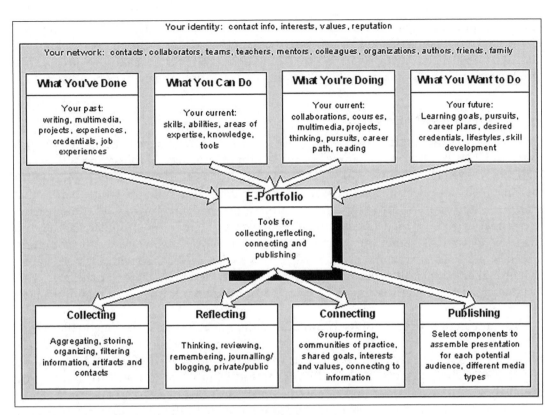

Areas that could be included in an ePortfolio

An example of a student's ePortfolio

and other files to be uploaded, as well as having a blog and wiki integrated and providing features for podcasting. Like most software that can be used for creating ePortfolios, Elgg allows content to be kept private, so that only designated users, such as a prospective employer or a teacher, can access the ePortfolio, and only with the owner's permission.

Interactive whiteboards

An **interactive whiteboard** (IWB) is made 'interactive' by being linked to a computer which uses special IWB software. The three essential components needed to use an IWB are the whiteboard itself, a computer which has IWB software installed and a **data projector** (or 'beamer') which projects the image from the computer screen onto the whiteboard. What makes the interactive whiteboard different from a normal whiteboard is that the teacher uses a special pen (or their finger with some makes of board) to manipulate content on the whiteboard itself, rather then using the mouse to manipulate images on the computer screen, which the teacher can also do. The latest IWBs can also be used with a wireless tablet PC (a smaller, hand-held computer) instead of a larger desktop or laptop computer. This has the added advantage that it can be passed around so that learners can manipulate the IWB from the tablet PC.

The interactive whiteboard itself comes in different sizes, measured diagonally across. The most common size is 190 cms (75 inches) across, and teachers tend to agree that the bigger the board the more effective it is, as images are more clearly displayed on a larger board. A whiteboard can be mobile (that is, moved from room to room) or fixed, but a mobile board needs to be set up again each time it is moved, which can take time. There are also backlit interactive whiteboards which do away with the need for a projector, but these are the most expensive kind of board. They are particularly useful in rooms with low ceilings.

The main advantage of an IWB used with a computer and data projector over a computer and data projector used on their own is that you can write on the IWB with your pen or finger and interact with what is on the screen from the front of the class rather than having to look down to your computer and using the mouse to control the screen.

IWBs in education

The British Council has been influential in bringing IWBs to language classrooms outside the UK, introducing them into Southeast Asia in 2003, and expanding their use of IWBs since then. In the UK itself, huge government investment from the early 1990s has seen IWBs appearing in primary and secondary schools, and further education, on a large scale. Both are examples of a top-down implementation of technology, with large organisations (in this case, the British Council and the British government) providing the impetus for the introduction of new tools in the classroom.

Excellent classroom work is being done using IWBs at primary, secondary and university level, as well as in the language classroom. Just Google 'IWB projects in schools', and you'll see a range of current and recent IWB projects in all sorts of school subjects. However, at the time of writing IWBs are being used mainly in large organisations like the British Council, or are part of government-led education initiatives, especially within the European Union. This is down to the high costs associated with IWBs. The hardware outlined above is expensive, and usually well beyond the budgets of individual language schools or education ministries in less wealthy countries. Although the costs of the hardware involved in using IWBs are expected to decrease over time, they are likely to remain beyond the reach of most EFL teachers worldwide for some time to come.

Using IWBs with learners

If you are lucky enough to have access to an IWB, you will know that the 'wow' effect is extremely high. In other words, IWBs look and sound impressive. Imagine a full-size colour screen in your classroom, with video, CD audio, pictures, interactive exercises like those found on a CD-ROM, access to the Internet, and more, all instantly accessible at the touch of your IWB pen. You can also use an IWB pen to write over the images on the screen, highlighting things in different colours, using a variety of fonts and styles to write in, or you can use the pen to hide and reveal images on the screen. Items can be moved around the screen using the pen, and previous lessons and content can easily be kept and retrieved, as everything is saved on the computer. This means that a huge bank of resources is always available at the touch of a pen.

The experiences and opinions of teachers who have used IWBs in the classroom tend to be positive. Teachers point to increased teacher and learner motivation through the introduction of a new (and impressive-looking) multimedia tool into the classroom – the 'wow' factor we mentioned earlier. Teachers also appreciate having so many multimedia tools available in one 'place' on the IWB. For example, at the touch of pen a teacher can play a section of an audio CD, bring up a transcript of the audio, highlight or underline part of it, make it disappear again while the audio is replayed, bring back the highlighted transcript, then move straight to a drag-and-drop activity based on the same transcript.

IWBs are particularly effective for the 'heads up' presentation stages in a lesson, as the teacher can have learners all looking at and concentrating on the screen at the same

A teacher activates an IWB with his finger

time. The teacher can also use content on the IWB to take the focus off themselves. This can be particularly useful for the modelling of language, for example the pronunciation of words or phrases. As IWBs can be connected to the Internet, excellent EFL-related or authentic content from a wide variety of sources can be accessed in seconds, and beamed up for the class to see. Another common use of IWBs is in conjunction with PowerPoint for presentations.

Research carried out into the impact of IWBs suggests that they can directly affect learners' motivation and attention levels, but that there is no direct correlation between heavy use of IWBs and increased test scores. This suggests that although learners may 'enjoy' IWBs as tools, there is no direct evidence to show that it actually improves their English. As with any new tool, it is as well to keep in mind some of the disadvantages associated with IWBs, namely their high cost and the fact that teacher training in how to use IWBs effectively is often ignored. As with any new tool, an IWB is only as good as the use that is made of it. There is a danger that IWB classes can become too teacher centred, with learners becoming a passive audience. However, as IWB manufacturers often point out, learners can also come up and use the IWB themselves, to move items around on the IWB and indeed direct a part of the lesson.

IWB materials and training

Initially there were very few materials available for IWBs in the field of TEFL. Mainstream primary and secondary education saw the development of IWB materials to teach science, maths, biology, geography, and so on, but the development of IWB software for the field of language teaching was slower to get off the ground. The early adopters of IWBs in ELT found it extremely time-consuming to produce their own IWB materials on the computer for use with classes, and publishers have responded to this by developing IWB software packages.

IWB teachers still can and do produce their own materials though, and these are typically electronic materials using tools such as those explored in Chapter 10, or any other material that can be displayed on a computer. Let's imagine a teacher who wants to use images of animals in danger of extinction for a lesson, and finds that the IWB software available in their school does not have any of these images. They simply go to an images site, such as Google images, or Flickr and download relevant images to the computer for display on the IWB. Similarly, a teacher may decide to use a specific activity which they have made in Hot Potatoes (see Chapter 10) on the IWB, for remedial work on a certain grammar point with the class. Some EFL publishers now produce IWB software to be used in conjunction with coursebooks. These are usually interactive versions of the coursebook itself, which can be displayed and manipulated on the IWB, rather than additional activities such as those traditionally found on coursebook related CD-ROMs.

Training for teachers in the use of a complex tool such as an IWB is important to ensure effective uptake. There is no point in a school spending considerable sums of money on an IWB if the teachers are unsure of how to use it or frightened of the technology. Large institutions which have taken IWBs on board on a large scale, like the British Council, will usually provide in-house training for their teachers, and several of the IWB manufacturers, such as Promethean in the UK, provide training and certification for IWB use, both face-to-face and online, as well as IWB software for mainstream school subjects. IWB suppliers provide online help and manuals for using IWBs, as well as short hands-on demonstrations of how IWBs can work in the classroom, either live or on video.

Conclusions | *In this chapter we have:*

- discussed the content found on CD-ROMs.
- considered how DVDs can be used in class.
- looked at ways of using CD-ROMs both during class time, and as a self-access tool.
- looked at how to evaluate CD-ROMs.
- considered computer-based testing for diagnostic testing, progress testing and officially recognised exams.
- examined the advantages and disadvantages of computer-based testing.
- considered ePortfolios (electronic portfolios).
- looked at interactive whiteboards (IWBs) – what they are, how to use them with learners and what materials and training are available for them.

ON THE CD-ROM YOU CAN LISTEN TO TWO TEACHERS TALKING ABOUT USING CD-ROMS AND THE INTERACTIVE WHITEBOARD, AND ALSO SEE AN INTERACTIVE WHITEBOARD IN ACTION.

Producing electronic materials

- What are electronic materials?
- Creating electronic materials online
- What is an authoring tool?
- Using authoring tools to produce materials

What are electronic materials?

When we refer to electronic materials creation and use in the context of this chapter, we are talking about informational resources, exercises and activities that you create yourself and which your students use on a computer as web page or CD-ROM content, or even in printed form. The production of these materials may include working with external web pages, using web page design skills, the use of small programs installed on your own computer or more complex CD-ROM production software. The choice of tool will be determined not only by the kinds of materials you want to produce, but also by the time available to you and the resources at your disposal. It is beyond the scope of this book to go into the more complex sides of materials production, so here we will mostly be concentrating on simple web-based materials or materials prepared using web resources.

Here we build on the word processing activities we covered in Chapter 2 and the use of websites in Chapter 3, and look at printable resources as well as on-screen interaction and activities shared over a computer network. To get a good idea of the kinds of materials we're considering in this section, take a look at the teaching resource from the Activities for ESL Students website (http://a4esl.org/) on the opposite page.

There are many reasons why you might want to create and use your own electronic materials in class. Firstly, you will be able to provide extra practice for weaker learners, and consolidation and review exercises for groups. Secondly, as you build up a collection of your own resources with your own learners' needs in mind, you will start to generate a large bank of materials which can be used in class or for self-study at any point in the future. In class these kinds of materials can provide a change of pace and can be highly motivating. Learners often enjoy the chance of competing against the computer with these kinds of discrete answer exercise types. If time is spent on feedback, you can check which language areas learners have had problems with and provide further practice materials if necessary.

A large school (or network of teachers) might even work electronic materials into a more collaborative project, building up a wide range of digital resources which are then shared between group members over a **server**. These may be adaptations of existing print materials in some cases, or completely new exercises. With the ready availability of web storage, these can be uploaded to a central repository, perhaps a wiki-based solution (see Chapter 7), or a more robust storage platform such as a **Virtual Learning Environment**

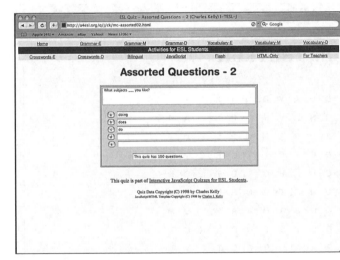

A The a4ESL homepage features a wide variety of exercises in many different categories (left-hand column) and in many different language combinations (right-hand column).

B A sample intermediate multiple-choice grammar exercise from the site. The learner is given a gapped sentence and has three choices with which to fill it. Feedback is given after each question, and a score is kept.

C A sample intermediate vocabulary crossword on animals, with clues down the right-hand side of the quiz grid itself. Learners type one letter in each gap in the grid.

(see Chapter 11) or a **Content Management System** (see Chapter 12). In many cases the wiki approach might be the ideal option, as it allows all contributors to work towards a final resource based on the 'rough copies' provided by the contributors, which can be added to and refined until the group is happy with the end result. These can then be downloaded by individuals, and customised to suit their particular teaching needs.

Creating electronic materials online

One of the easiest ways of getting started in this area is to use some of the simple exercise generators which can be found online. These produce a variety of exercises, from printable resources to be taken into class to exercises which can be turned into web pages and made available on the Internet, both for your learners and for other teachers if you decide you want to share them. One of the most popular is the Discovery School Puzzlemaker (http://puzzlemaker.school.discovery.com/). This features a variety of different exercise types, including traditional ones such as word searches.

In this case you have to print out the page and photocopy it for your class. You could export the content to Word which would allow you to add images of fruit to the task.

Puzzle makers are ideal tools for reviewing vocabulary, and take the hard work out of preparing many different quick quizzes. In addition, you can give your students the opportunity to prepare quizzes themselves using these tools. Another useful tool is Smile (http://smile.clear.msu.edu). This tool allows you to create a free account in which to manage your own online bank of exercises with student tracking and a good variety of exercise types. Here you can choose from multiple choice, true/false, drag and drop, sentence mix, paragraph mix, cloze and multiple select. Activities are created online and can be done by learners entirely online, although some, such as cloze texts, are suitable for printing out and doing offline. This is an ideal site for exam preparation classes. One of the major advantages of a site like this is that it allows you to build up a manageable collection of exercises, making it easier to address the individual problems of particular learners, but also to make consistent use of web-based exercises throughout the duration of a course. This will help to give your learners an idea of why they are being introduced to these materials, and also give them a good overview of what they are covering online. The subject of learner tracking and Learner Management Systems is dealt with in greater detail in Chapter 11.

What is an authoring tool?

An authoring tool is an installable program that allows you to create materials in electronic format which can then be distributed on a CD-ROM, DVD, USB pen drive, floppy disc or via a web page to your learners. Authoring programs are used to make CD-ROM-based reference tools like Microsoft Encarta (see Chapter 8), but also more simple resources like information leaflets, brochures, handouts and interactive exercises.

Most teachers will perhaps not have a need for the more expensive and professional solutions, although any centre involved in blended learning solutions (see Chapter 11) which use custom-developed materials might be well-advised to look at digital content development as a viable way of making interactive and multimedia-based materials available to its learners. As with a lot of high-end technology, it should be borne in mind that the learning curve for a lot of these packages is steep, and that proficient production will have a significant drain on both financial and staffing resources during the developmental phase.

Authoring tools usually feature a simple design interface, with drag-and-drop elements allowing you to add pictures, sounds and video material to the screen, along with navigational options such as forward and back arrows, and content menus. Some of the more professional authoring tools have complex programming languages allowing you to control what happens in greater detail, but these will require a degree of expert knowledge which most teachers will probably not have the time or inclination to acquire. Therefore you would be well-advised to ensure that any software you choose is going to be useful to you. This can be done by downloading and installing trial versions before making any purchasing decisions.

If you would like to explore the commercial side of multimedia creation, you may like to look at Mediator (http://www.matchware.com/en/products/mediator/edu/why.htm), Macromedia Director (http://www.adobe.com/products/director/) or Neobook (http://www.neosoftware.com/nbw.html). Here we will be considering free or reasonably-priced resources for content creation, allowing you to experiment without spending any or very much money.

Using authoring tools to produce materials

Perhaps the most famous authoring tool in our field is Hot Potatoes. This is a small Windows or Mac program that creates a variety of exercises and can be freely downloaded for educational purposes (http://hotpot.uvic.ca/). This program will install on your own computer and allow you to create web-based exercises of the following types:

- multiple choice
- short answer
- jumbled sentence
- crossword
- matching/ordering
- gap-fill

It also allows you to include audio files in MP3 format and will even allow you to store your exercises on a central server so that they can be accessed from anywhere with an Internet connection. To get started, install the program and find it in your program folder. When you first start it up you will be presented with the following screen.

From here you can choose one of the tools. Let's take a look at creating a simple exercise. Click on JQuiz to get started (see page 131 top). Here you can put the title of the exercise, and start by adding question 1. There are four answers to my first question, each with their own feedback, and answer B is marked as the correct one (see page 131 bottom). Now click the up arrow next to Q1 on the screen and add a second question, with answers and feedback. Don't forget to mark the correct answer. Continue doing this until you have made your quiz.

Now it's time to actually create the quiz as a web page. First make sure you save your quiz so that you can return to it later to make edits if you need to (File – Save). Now we will turn this into an interactive web page. Click on 'File – Create Web page' and then choose the 'Webpage for v6 browsers' option. Give the filename and then save it. You should now be able to look at it in a web browser.

JQuiz: [Untitled]

File   Edit   Insert   Manage Questions   Options   Help

| Title | **Gavin's Quiz** |

Q 1   What is the capital of England?   Multiple-choice

	Answers	**Feedback**	**Settings**
A	Paris	No, that's in France.	☐ Correct
B	London	Correct! With a population of....	☑ Correct
C	Barcelona	No, that's in Spain (and it's not the capital either).	☐ Correct
D	Rome	Rome is the capital of Italy - so it's not that one.	☐ Correct

Config: english6.cfg

| Title | **Gavin's Quiz** |

Q 2   What is the capital of Spain?   Multiple-choice

	Answers	**Feedback**	**Settings**
A	Barcelona	No - that's in Spain, but it's not the capital.	☐ Correct
B	Sevilla	A very beautiful city in Andalucia - but it's not the capital.	☐ Correct
C	Madrid	Yes! Madrid is in the centre of Spain, and it's the capital, with a population of...	☑ Correct
D	Granada	It's famous for the Moorish palace called the Alhambra - but it's not the capital.	☐ Correct

Config: english6.cfg

That's how the bare bones of all the quizzes generated by Hot Potatoes work. If you want to delve deeper into things like formatting the output, changing colours, and so on, then you should look in the Options menu when you are creating a quiz, or investigate the 'Help' file that comes with the program. There are also plenty of tutorial examples on the Hot Potatoes website (http://hotpot.uvic.ca/tutorials6.htm).

Once you have created a set of exercises, you can package them all together using 'The Masher'. This is a utility accessed from the start page of the Hot Potatoes program which will guide you through linking a set of individual items into a small learning package, with full navigation between the various elements. You can then distribute these on discs, or memory sticks or CD-ROMs, or put them on a website if you or your school has one.

Interactive stories

Another area to explore in electronic materials, and a move away from straightforward test and practice exercises, is the creation of interactive stories where learners read scenarios and then make choices to decide what they will do at certain key points. These are excellent for reading comprehension practice or as small-group discussions that encourage collaborative and critical thinking skills. They encourage learners to develop a wide range of skills from listening to debating, agreeing and disagreeing and making points and supporting them. Since these are basically text-driven activities, you should be able to produce them for any level. You can see some examples of typical interactive stories (or reading mazes) here (http://www.halfbakedsoftware.com/quandary/version_2/examples/).

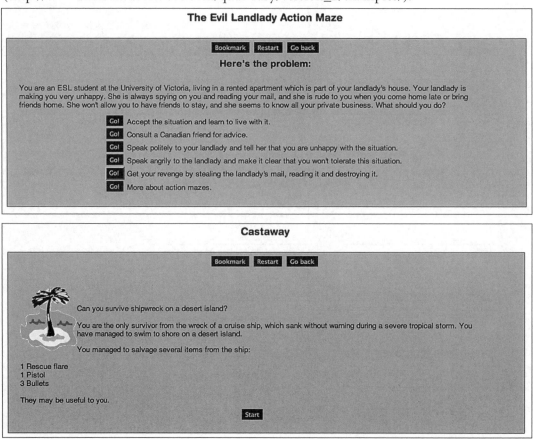

In the examples on the opposite page, the reader is presented with a scenario and a set of choices on each screen. Each time a choice is made the story unfolds further. The Evil Landlady Action Maze is based around the scenario of an ESL student at a Canadian university who is having problems with her landlady, while the Castaway Maze involves learners in a struggle for survival on a desert island. This desert island scenario in particular is a familiar language practice tool, presented in a slightly different way.

The examples below were made with a piece of software called Quandary. A demonstration version of the software is available (http://www.halfbakedsoftware.com/ quandary.php), and provides enough information for you to get an idea of whether the software is useful to you or not. Download the demo version from the Half Baked Software site above. Note that the full program costs $50 at the time of writing. Here's how it works:

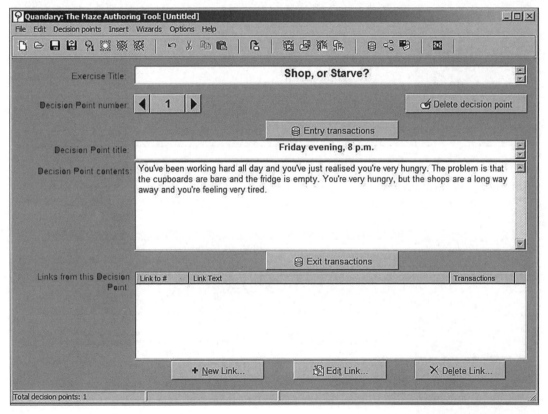

You need to give your reading maze a title (Exercise Title) and then give the opening screen a title (Decision Point title). Now start by describing the opening scenario of your maze (Decision Point contents). The idea now is to add two (or more) choices from this opening screen and further screens where the story will develop. Click on '+ New Link'. Select 'Create a new decision point' and give it a relevant title. Do this for the choices you want to offer your learners. In our example on the next page (top), they can decide to go shopping or wait until tomorrow.

Notice that the 'Go shopping' option is now automatically linked to Decision Point 2 and 'Wait till tomorrow' is linked to Decision Point 3. Use the forward arrow next to the Decision Point number to advance to Decision Point 2 and add the text for that option. Do

Exercise Title: Shop, or Starve?

Decision Point number: ◀ 1 ▶   🖋 Delete decision point

🗄 Entry transactions

Decision Point title: Friday evening, 8 p.m.

Decision Point contents: You've been working hard all day and you've just realised you're very hungry. The problem is that the cupboards are bare and the fridge is empty. You're very hungry, but the shops are a long way away and you're feeling very tired. What will you do?

🗄 Exit transactions

Links from this Decision Point

Link to #	Link Text	Transactions
2	Go shopping	
3	Wait till tomorrow	

✚ New Link...   🗐 Edit Link...   ✕ Delete Link...

Total decision points: 3

the same with Decision Point 3. Now you will have an opening screen with two options, each linked to another screen (see below). When you have finished your small maze, save it (File – Save File) and then convert it to a web-based activity for your learners. You can

Exercise Title: Shop, or Starve?

Decision Point number: ◀ 2 ▶   🖋 Delete decision point

🗄 Entry transactions

Decision Point title: Go shopping

Decision Point contents: You decide to go shopping. It's late, so you'll have to go to an out-of-town shop. The problem is you've got no money for the bus. You could walk, but it would take hours.

🗄 Exit transactions

Links from this Decision Point

Link to #	Link Text	Transactions
4	Walk to the shop	
5	Go to bed hungry	

✚ New Link...   🗐 Edit Link...   ✕ Delete Link...

Total decision points: 5

do this by clicking 'File', then 'Export to XHTML'. When it has finished, you will be able to preview it in your browser.

These are just a couple of options for creating online materials. Indeed the area of online materials covers such a wide variety of formats and storage options that we are really only able to scratch the surface here. Exploring some of the sites and programs we have covered here will help to give you an idea of the kinds of things that can be produced with very little technical knowledge (designed, as the majority are, by teachers rather than technicians), but you will probably want to search further to get an idea of the bigger picture. Make sure that you brush up on your search skills from Chapter 3 before venturing on to see what's out there. To get you started, here are a few more examples:

Clarity Software (http://www.clarityenglish.com/)

Clarity has a long history in producing English language related products, and their authoring tools are both reasonably priced and easy to use. Have a look at their Author Plus Pro and Tense Buster programs, which can be used for a variety of different exercise types, including audio, graphics and video content, and allow for the creation of listening comprehension exercises, interactive dictations and presentations. It also has a sophisticated learner tracking option, allowing you to see your learners' progress through the materials.

Creative Technology – Software for Teaching
(http://www.cict.co.uk/software/textoys/index.htm)

Features Quandary and other useful tools including a marking program for incorporating into Word (Chapter 2), a cloze program called WebRhubarb and a text reconstruction program called WebSequitor, where learners reconstruct written texts from smaller chunks. These are all good programs, produced by the lead developer of the Hot Potatoes suite we looked at above.

QUIA (http://www.quia.com/subscription/)

This is a subscription-based service allowing for the creation of various types of activities, surveys and web pages, as well as extensive learner tracking options. The site offers a variety of ready-made templates for materials creation and the ability to set up a study space for your learners, as well as access to over two million activities already in the library.

Conclusions | *In this chapter we have:*

- considered various types of interactive exercises.
- looked at websites which allow for the creation of interactive exercises.
- examined reasons for using interactive exercises with learners.
- learnt how to produce a variety of exercise types.
- produced an interactive reading maze.

> ON THE CD-ROM YOU CAN HEAR TWO TEACHERS TALKING ABOUT HOW THEY CREATE THEIR OWN MATERIALS AND WATCH A TUTORIAL ON USING HOT POTATOES.

e-learning: online teaching and training

- **What is e-learning?**
- **Teaching and learning online**
- **Course design for online learning: examples**
- **Course design for online learning: considerations**
- **How to get started with online learning**
- **Teacher training and online learning**
- **Discussion lists and online groups**

What is e-learning?

So far we have looked mainly at the use of technology to enhance courses where the classroom and face-to-face contacts are the main element. Here we look specifically at online teaching and learning, that is teaching and learning done mainly at a distance, usually via a personal computer and the Internet. We have already looked at some of the tools that can be used as part of an online course, for example online reference tools in Chapter 8.

e-learning refers to learning that takes place using technology, such as the Internet, CD-ROMs and portable devices like mobile phones or MP3 players. There are several terms associated with e-learning, which are often used interchangeably and which can be rather confusing. Let's take a quick look at some of the main terms here:

- **Distance learning**
  The term *distance learning* originally applied to traditional paper-based distance courses delivered by mail. Nowadays distance learning includes learning via technology such as the Internet, CD-ROMs and mobile technologies (see Chapter 12), hence the newer term *e-learning*. *Distance* or *e-learning* are often used as umbrella names for the terms below.

- **Open learning**
  This is one aspect of distance learning and simply refers to how much independence the learner has. The more open a distance course is, the more autonomy the learner has in deciding what course content to cover, how to do so and when.

- **Online learning**
  This is learning which takes place via the Internet. As such, online learning is a facet of e-learning.

- **Blended learning**
  This is a mixture of online and face-to-face course delivery. For example, learners might meet once a week with a teacher face-to-face for an hour, and do a further two hours' work weekly online. In some situations the digital element is done offline with a CD-ROM.

Teaching and learning online

How does online learning actually work in practice? The following scenarios are examples of learning situations which make use of the computer, but they are not necessarily all examples of online learning.

- Learners in a self-study centre, or at home, use a CD-ROM which provides them with extra practice of what they have done in class.

- During class, learners are taken to a computer room, and do exercises on a language website on the Internet, in pairs.

- Learners use an ICT tool, such as blogs, wikis, chat or podcasts, for project work, either inside or outside the classroom.

- Learners email their homework or class assignment to the teacher, who marks it and emails it back to learners.

- The teacher uses a blog to provide learners with online links for reading and listening, homework assignments, and summaries of classwork for learners who miss class.

- The classroom is equipped with an interactive whiteboard, which is regularly used in class.

- Learners meet face-to-face only once a month, and do classwork using email, chat, phone and shared activities on the Internet.

We would argue that only the last scenario above is an example of online learning. In fact, in this case, as the learners do meet face-to-face, we are talking about blended learning, a mixture of online and face-to-face course delivery.

Key to the concept of online learning is that a very significant part of the course delivery and coursework takes place virtually, using the Internet. At one end of the scale we have a 100 percent online course, where learners never meet face-to-face, and all course content and coursework takes place online, and at the other end of the scale, a blended option where most coursework takes place face-to-face, but there is a regular and carefully integrated online component to the course.

Online learning is often delivered via a learning 'platform' or **Virtual Learning Environment** (VLE). Also known as a **Learner Management System** (LMS), or a virtual classroom, a VLE is a web-based platform on which course content can be stored. It is accessed by learners on the Internet, and they can not only see course content, such as documents, audio and video lectures, but also do activities such as quizzes, questionnaires and tests, or use communication tools like discussion forums or text and audio chat. Newer VLEs even integrate blogs and wikis. Increasingly popular in the VLE world is Moodle, an open source VLE which is free. Other well-known VLEs are WebCT, which recently merged with Blackboard, and First Class, although neither of these is free.

The advantage of a VLE for course delivery is that everything is in one place, and most VLEs provide **tracking facilities**, so that the online tutor can see who has logged in when, and see what activities learners have done, or what documents and forums they have accessed. VLEs also usually provide fairly sophisticated tools for assessment and grading, with records kept for each learner. Thus a teacher can evaluate a learner's written work or assignments in the VLE, as well as their contributions to forums, and these grades are automatically recorded. Results for automatically graded activities (like quizzes or tests) will also be fed into the learners 'grade book' with the learner able to consult their grades and check progress at any point. With this combination of automatically graded activities and tutor assessment, VLEs provide a much richer tool for learner evaluation than, for example, a CD-ROM, where learner assessment will normally be based on automatic grading only.

Course design for online learning: examples

What might an online course look like? Let's look at some examples.

Course 1: A 100 percent online language learning course

This course is likely to be instigated by an institution in response to a perceived demand in the market, or perhaps as part of a government-sponsored initiative. The course is not unlike a coursebook online, with ten units covering the four skills (reading, listening, writing and speaking), grammar and vocabulary. Learners work their way through a series of materials and activities online, which include reading and listening texts, and writing, grammar and vocabulary activities. Many of the activities are self-marking, with feedback given automatically by the computer, but activities such as writing texts are sent to a tutor via email. Speaking is dealt with via a phone or Skype tutorial every unit (see Chapter 6), and learners also need to send regular voice mail to their tutor. The course can be taken by an individual learner, who works through the course materials at their own pace, or by small groups of learners, who all start at the same time, and have set deadlines for work. For example, learners need to complete one unit per month, and certain activities within that unit by specified dates in the month. In the case of a small group, additional facilities like online forums and a text/audio chat room are provided for group members to discuss issues and materials, and to meet in regularly, with and without a tutor.

Course 2: A blended language learning course

A language learning course delivered 75 percent online and 25 percent face-to-face. This course is similar to Course 1 in that it is likely to be instigated by an institution in response to a perceived demand in the market or as part of a government-sponsored initiative, but learners meet once a month face-to-face in a group with a teacher. Similar materials to those found in Course 1 covering the four skills, grammar and vocabulary are delivered both online and face-to-face, but speaking activities are carried out mainly face-to-face. Phone contact and Skype may provide extra speaking practice for learners on this course.

Course 3: A face-to-face language learning course with additional online materials

A typical language learning course, which uses online tools to support and extend face-to-face lessons. Strictly speaking this is not an online course, but it is the way most teachers get involved in online learning and become more confident with using online tools with their learners at a distance. The teacher uses the following online tools:

- a tutor blog to provide extra reading and listening practice, to set homework and to provide summaries of class work.
- Learners email the teacher all class assignments, which are returned via email.
- The teacher offers regular chat session via Skype for the learners, outside class time, for example every second weekend at a specific time, for an hour.
- The teacher does project work with the class involving ICT tools like blogs, wikis or podcasts, and encourages learners to work on these projects outside class time, in virtual groups.

Typically, a teacher with a personal interest in integrating technology into their classes will start off with a Course 3 approach, but the reality is that many teachers are increasingly finding themselves in the position of being asked or told to use a Course 1 or Course 2 approach as part of an institution-wide online learning initiative. In this situation, it is essential for the teacher to have a clear grasp of the fundamentals of online course design as well as an overview of the kinds of tools and software available, including their limitations, many of which we have explored in previous chapters.

A tutor blog summarising a recent class and providing links for extra out-of-class work.

Course design for online learning: considerations

In designing online learning courses, there are certain questions which the course designer or individual teacher needs to consider carefully if the courses are to be of good quality. If you are thinking of trying out elements of online learning with your own learners, or are involved in larger scale online learning projects, the list of questions below will help you to bear in mind some of the key considerations. For a course or study programme to demonstrate good practice in online learning, the following questions need to be answered satisfactorily at the design stage.

Delivery mode

- Is the course purely online, or does it include blended learning? If blended, exactly what percentage of the course takes place face-to-face, and how often do learners meet?

- What elements of the course content are delivered online, and what elements are delivered face-to-face?

- How exactly are the online components of the course delivered? By email and chat? In a VLE? Via an ad hoc collection of online tools like Skype, email and Yahoo! Groups?

- Can a CD-ROM provide a useful means of delivering digital content for elements that are difficult to download, for example video content?

- Is the method of delivery suited to the content? In other words, if an online course promises to teach and practise pronunciation, but the delivery mode is via email, it is unlikely to work!

- What elements of the course will take place synchronously, that is, in real time, and what elements asynchronously, that is, not in real time? What synchronous and asynchronous tools will be used?

- Does the course content and delivery mode reflect the learners' needs?

Task design and materials

- What materials will be used for the course content? Will they be tailor-made content and activities, or will existing resources on the Internet be used?

- What issues of copyright need to be taken into account, if you are using existing activities, graphics and websites available on the Internet?

- Is content attractively presented and varied, for example with graphics and animation? Is there a range of media used – audio, video, text – and a range of tools – forums, text/audio chat, email, voice mail?

- Are different task types provided? For example, are all the grammar exercises drag-and-drop or are various activity types available?

- Do task types appeal to a variety of learner styles?
- Are there plenty of opportunities for interaction between learners, and between learners and tutors, built into the tasks and overall course design?

Learners

- Are the learners computer literate, or will they need training to use the online tools? If training is needed, how will this be provided?
- To what extent are the learners prepared for and suitable for e-learning? How will their course expectations be dealt with?
- Will the course be individual self-study, or will learners work through the course material at the same time, in small groups? What is the maximum size for a group?
- If the course is 100 percent online and group-based, how and when will group formation and socialising activities be integrated? How will learners be made to feel part of an online learning group?
- How much tutor support, and access to tutors, will learners be given?

Teacher/Tutors

- Are the tutors experienced in e-learning, as well as computer literate, or will they need training to deliver the course? If training is needed, how will this be provided?
- To what extent will tutors be involved in course design, or will they simply deliver the course?
- What is the ratio of learners to tutors, and how many hours a week are tutors expected to work on the online component of a course?
- How much support are tutors given, and by whom?

Assessment and evaluation

- How will the success – or otherwise – of the course itself be evaluated?
- Will the course be evaluated as it is running (known as 'formative assessment') or only at the end ('summative assessment')?
- How will learners' coursework be assessed and graded?
- How will tutors' performance be evaluated?

As we see above, many of the issues involved in online instructional design are not dissimilar to the considerations for putting together a face-to-face course, where we also need to ensure that course content meets our learners' needs, caters to a range of learning styles and has evaluation procedures in place. One of the keys to effective online course delivery, though, is that the tools chosen for the tasks match the aims of the activity and course.

How to get started with online learning

If you are new to online learning, but would like to experiment with it, as with anything new it's a good idea to start small. The examples using simple online tools in the **Course 3** scenario above are a good way to start. If you are teaching adults, it is useful to first discuss with your learners themselves whether they would like to have an online component added to their face-to-face course. Many adults spend a lot of time in front of a computer at their workplace, and may not see the point of spending extra time out of class doing more work in front of one. Others value the social elements of their language classes, and may not enjoy communication with their peers which is not face-to-face. Only if you can convince your learners (and yourself) of the added value that online learning can bring to their language learning, should you try it out. Your learners' needs, likes and learning goals need to be taken into account to avoid the gratuitous application of online learning for its own sake, which will only alienate learners.

In the case of secondary school learners, many of them will already be familiar with Internet tools like blogs, wikis and chat, and will probably embrace the use of technology in the classroom more readily than adults. As with using any new tool with learners, it is useful to find out what level of expertise and experience younger learners already have with any tools you may want to introduce into your teaching.

If you are involved in a scenario more like **Course 1** or **Course 2** above, our first piece of advice is that, if you can, you should do a course online yourself, as a learner. This does not necessarily need to be a language course, but could be in an area that you are interested in (cooking, photography or linguistics, for example) or a teacher development course online. Research, as well as anecdotal evidence, suggests that effective online tutors usually have previous experience as online learners. Certainly being an online learner oneself is the fastest and most effective way of getting insights into the online learning and teaching process, as well as familiarity with the tools and software available.

If you are involved in a scenario such as **Course 1** (100 percent online), special attention needs to be paid to the development of group dynamics online and to online socialisation processes.

Probably one of the most important things for teachers and institutions who get involved in online learning is to realise that online learning is not a cheap and easy alternative to face-to-face learning. Quite the opposite, in fact. The more effective an online course is, the more time it has been given, at the design and development stages and also during the tutoring stage. Just ask anyone with any online tutoring experience whether they think face-to-face teaching or online tutoring is more time-consuming! In the online context, individual learners often have unlimited access to their tutors by email, and this may result in learners having unrealistic expectations of their tutors in terms of response time and availability. It's always a good idea to clearly establish from the outset how long a tutor will take to respond to learners' online work or emails. A 24- to 48-hour turnaround time is often stipulated. If synchronous access to tutors is included in a course, for example via Skype, the tutor can specify 'office hours' when they are available for audio (or text) chat.

Finally, here is a summary of tips to keep in mind if you are considering working with online learning. The tips below refer mainly to 100 percent online courses, but several of them will be relevant to blended courses as well.

- Take an online course. Experiencing online learning yourself will make you much more aware of – and empathetic to – difficulties your own online learners may encounter, as well as issues of online group dynamics, the importance of contact with the tutor, and so on.

- Ensure that all design and delivery issues are resolved at the planning stage. See the checklist above. Be prepared to spend a lot of time on course preparation and on tutoring.

- Find out about your learners' expectations about the online course, and deal with any unrealistic expectations, early on.

- Create interactive tasks at the beginning of your online course to introduce the learners to the technicalities of the online environment if you are using a VLE.

- Create an online community by providing opportunities for learners to interact with each other and to get to know each other socially from the very beginning of the course.

- Create spaces, communication channels and norms for dealing with issues and conflict. This can be done both publicly and privately, and should be available throughout the course.

- Establish norms, protocols or guidelines for group interaction and behaviour. These can be negotiated by participants or provided by you. Provide clear guidelines as to tutor roles, contact times and turnaround time for responding to work and emails.

- Allow for group closure by, for example, celebrating achievements, disseminating products, providing feedback, designing 'closing' activities and providing for post-course contact and development.

Teacher training and online learning

So far we have been looking at online courses for learners. Let's now turn our attention to online courses and professional development groups for teachers. With increasing access to the Internet, teachers, too, can find opportunities for professional development which do not involve expensive courses or travel. Any search in Google using combinations of words like 'teaching English', 'TEFL', 'Certificate', 'online' and 'training' will bring up links to a wealth of online courses, certificates, diplomas and degrees for teachers. Online training courses on offer include:

- short methodology courses for teachers, for example Teaching Young Learners, Teaching Listening or Using Drama in the Classroom.

- pre-service certificate courses.

- in-service diploma courses, for example the Trinity Diploma or Cambridge ESOL DELTA.

- MAs and university diplomas.

Some of these courses are offered by established and reputable training bodies or academic institutions. Others are not. Some are examples of good practice in online learning. Others are not. How does the teacher who wishes to pursue professional development at a distance, whether via a formal accredited academic course, or a shorter teacher development course, distinguish between what are and what are not valid training courses? The obvious answer is that for more formal and academic courses ensure that the course is accredited by a recognised body, while for more informal courses, make sure the course providers are known and respected in the field. Also, make sure that the course's purported aims are in fact compatible with online delivery. For example, any pre-service teaching course which is delivered fully online is likely to lack credibility, as observed face-to-face teaching practice is a usual requirement of these courses.

Quite apart from the issue of accreditation and validation, online training courses also need to demonstrate current best practice in the field of online learning. Our checklist of issues on course design above can help you decide whether an online training course is actually any good in terms of content and delivery. To choose an online course, you should have clear answers to most of the issues raised in the course design section, either via the course web page, or in email correspondence with the course providers.

For the teacher who does not wish to embark on a course, but would like to keep up-to-date with issues in the field, or develop their skills more informally, there are number of options online. You could join or set up an online discussion group, subscribe to blogs or podcasts, or read online journals or magazines. In the next section we will look specifically at online discussion lists and groups, and how these might help with teacher development.

Discussion lists and online groups

You will have probably come across terms like 'mailing list', 'discussion group', 'Yahoo group' or others to describe groups of people connected by a common professional interest like teaching or teacher training who are in contact with each other via email. As is often the case with these terms, they tend to be used interchangeably, although there are in fact some differences, which we should clarify.

A **mailing list** is the simplest form of email communication, and is informative. Typically a mailing list disseminates information, for example on forthcoming online courses or conferences, or new materials or articles, to those who sign up and join the list. One example is the British Council's ELTECS lists, which keep members around the world informed of events, activities, courses and grants (http://www.britishcouncil.org/eltecs-join.htm). A mailing list is best compared to a snail mail, or normal mail, newsletter, which members receive regularly, and which keeps them up-to-date.

A **discussion list** is similar to a mailing list but will allow for and encourage discussion of topics and issues. A lot of these are run using mailing list software called Listserv or Majordomo, and are based in universities around the world. Two very popular ones are TESL-L (http://www.hunter.cuny.edu/~tesl-l/) and NETEACH-L (http://hunter.listserv.cuny.edu/archives/neteach-l.html). Messages from a discussion list are sent to members by email. They are not viewed on the Internet, although there is usually a searchable archive of past messages available on a server.

A **discussion group** is similar to a discussion list, and uses not only email but typically also offers a location online where documents, files and photos can be stored, and perhaps other facilities for members, such as text chat, a calendar and access to a member database. On the opposite page is a screenshot of a well-known discussion group site, Yahoo! Groups. On the left-hand side of the screen you can see the various facilities that this particular discussion group offers. Members who join this group can have the messages posted by

YAHOO! GROUPS   Sign In   New User? Sign Up   Groups Home · Help

ttedsig · IATEFL TTEd SIG

	Home
Home	
Messages	[Join This Group!]
Members Only	**Activity within 7 days:** 1 New Member · 2 New Messages
Post	
Files	**Description**
Photos	This is the official list of the IATEFL Teacher Trainers and Educators Special Interest Group (TTEd SIG). Make sure that you visit the list's website at:
Links	
Database	http://www.ihes.com/ttsig
Polls	
Members	**Most Recent Messages** (View All) Search: [_____] [Search] Advanced **Start Topic**
Calendar	(Group by Topic)
Promote	

Info   Settings

Group Information

Members: 545
Category: College and University
Founded: Jun 29, 2001
Language: English

Trainer Development Courses
Hello Trainers, I'm not sure if it is kosher to "advertise" on this list, but it seems obvious that some of you would be pleased to know about some really
Posted · Wed Dec 13, 2006 1:16 pm

Susan Barduhn
susanbarduhn
☺ Offline
✉ Send Email

Request for assistance
Dear Colleagues, A request for help with MA research regarding `teachers adapting to new contexts and roles' Could you spare some time to complete a brief
Posted · Mon Dec 11, 2006 8:17 pm

darrenrelliott
☺ Offline
✉ Send Email

BBC I British Council teaching English newsletter 29 Nov 06
29 November, 2006 Hello and welcome to the newsletter for the BBC I British Council site, Teaching English. This week we have a number of new resources for

Nik Peachey
nik.peachey@...
✉ Send Email

other group members sent to them either as individual emails or in one daily digest email, or members can decide to receive no email, and to only view messages by visiting the Yahoo! group site itself.

IATEFL (The International Association of Teachers of English as a Foreign Language) has several discussion groups which use Yahoo! Groups, based around individual Special Interest Groups (SIGs), such as teacher trainers, teaching young learners, testing and assessment, learning technologies, and so on (http://www.iatefl.org).

Mailing and discussion lists and groups are simply ways in which groups of people with common interests use email to communicate. As we have seen above, the main differences between different types of lists and groups is between how much discussion/interaction takes place, and what tools are available to members. There is, however, another sort of group in which not only is there a lot of discussion and interaction between members but also shared responsibilities, tasks and activities. These groups are known as **communities of practice**, or CoPs for short. When a CoP is an online group, it is called a 'distributed' CoP. Two exemplary CoPs in the teaching profession are the Webheads group and the Dogme group, both of which use Yahoo! Groups to communicate, and both of which we highly recommend joining.

- **Webheads** (http://www.webheads.info/)
  These are a group of ESL/EFL teachers and trainers from around the world, who discuss how to use technology with their classes. Members try out various technologies and tools with their own classes, make contact with other Webhead classes by using ICT tools like chat, blogs and wikis, and then discuss how these impact on their own classroom practice.

- **Dogme** (http://groups.yahoo.com/group/dogme/)
  These are a group of teachers, trainers and materials writers interested in exploring how to teach without using materials like coursebooks, and using the learners themselves as resources to generate content and dialogue. Like Webheads, Dogme members often try things out in class, then discuss them afterwards with the group.

Both of these groups display the characteristics of CoPs outlined below.

- Belonging to the CoP is voluntary.

- Goals for the group are negotiated by the members. For example, a CoP of secondary school teachers might as a group decide to examine, discuss and work with the issue of discipline in their classes for a month.

- Some roles in a CoP are assigned (for example, Person X always uploads files for the group); other roles are emergent (for example, Person Y is an expert on topic 1, and Person Z is an expert on topic 2, and depending on which topic is under discussion, Y or Z will play a leading role).

- The CoP will produce artefacts, or 'resources', like guidelines or PowerPoint presentations, which will be archived for the group to access.

- The issues discussed by the group will be put into practice by group members. For example, if the group discusses an issue like discipline in class, members will then try out specific discipline strategies with their own classes.

- The CoP will engage in overt reflection about what they are doing – what works well and what doesn't, and why and how practice can be improved.

- Usually a CoP will have several core members who contribute regularly to discussions, and many more boundary members, who may follow discussions but not take part. These boundary members may well take what they learn in one CoP to another CoP.

Most teachers involved in online development will belong to several mailing lists and discussion groups, and each list or group will usually display its own characteristics. Some online teachers' groups, like the Webheads and Dogme groups described above, have a constant stream of messages, which can add up to hundreds of messages per month. Others, like the ELTECS lists, will have a couple of messages a day, usually consisting of information about forthcoming events and projects related to the EFL/ESL profession. Still others, like some of the IATEFL SIG groups, may lie dormant for months, then are very busy for a period of weeks as a planned discussion on a certain topic is held. None of these different types of lists or groups is inherently 'better' than any other. It's simply a matter of each teacher joining those groups they feel will be of most benefit to them. We belong to over 30 discussion lists and groups between us!

One way of dealing with the inevitably large amounts of email generated by belonging to several online discussion lists or groups is to have your subscription to the group set to receiving only one daily digest email per day, or to no mail, so that you regularly visit the site itself to read messages.

As we have seen, the Internet brings a wealth of opportunities to the teacher and teacher trainer for continuous professional development, as well as for contact with other teachers around the world with similar concerns and interests. One way of keeping up with developments in our field is to belong to at least some of the groups we mentioned in this chapter.

Conclusions | *In this chapter we have:*

- defined some of the terms connected with e-learning.
- looked at examples of online courses for learners of English.
- considered what needs to be taken into account when designing an online course.
- looked at how to get started with offering online courses to learners.
- discussed online teacher training courses.
- discussed other professional development opportunities for teachers online, such as belonging to mailing lists, discussion groups and online (distributed) communities of practice.

 ON THE CD-ROM YOU CAN HEAR A TEACHER TALKING ABOUT PROFESSIONAL DEVELOPMENT AND WATCH A TUTORIAL ABOUT JOINING WEBHEADS.

Preparing for the future

- **The state of the art**
- **How to keep up-to-date**
- **Web 2.0**
- **The future of online learning**
- **Virtual learning**
- **m-learning**

The state of the art

In the ten years that we have been training teachers to use technology in ELT, the pace of change has been slow. However, there are signs now that the pace is beginning to accelerate with the advent of more user-friendly tools and software, and greater opportunities for more formalised training. Indeed, it is rare these days for any teacher not to have made some small investment in the use of technology in their work, from the teacher who uses a word processor to put together worksheets to the more active users who are members of online communities of practice groups.

One of the main entry points into technology for a lot of teachers has been their own experience of it in the form of distance training, with more and more busy professionals finding themselves only having the time and resources to develop professionally by taking advantage of online courses in teacher education – from short skills-based courses to the longer in-service training like the distance learning version of the DELTA. Courses like these have obliged many teachers to engage more with technology, which has resulted in a change of attitude. Rather than learning technology skills in isolation, they have seen at first hand how technology can enhance training, and these experiences have permeated their own professional practice.

In general secondary and primary education, one of the more remarkable success stories has been the uptake of interactive whiteboards (IWBs). The UK state primary and secondary sector, for example, has an average of 7.5 IWBs per school to date, and the UK is the biggest market for IWBs in the world, with sales in 2004 being eighty times higher than in Germany. Elsewhere, the Enciclomedia project in Mexico aims to provide over 13,000 elementary schools with IWBs and Internet connectivity in the long term. Yet government funded projects on this scale are still remarkably rare, in part at least because of the high installation costs.

The success of this technology is largely due to the fact that it uses a very familiar metaphor – the board – and consigns the computer to a secondary or almost invisible role in the classroom. This is a role envisaged by Stephen Bax in his article 'CALL – Past, Present and Future', where he suggests that technology needs to become 'invisible', to both the teacher and the learner, in order to be fully integrated into the learning process. It needs to become as natural a part of the classroom as more traditional, longer-established 'tools' like the coursebook or dictionary. His article is available online (http://www.iateflcompsig. org.uk/media/callpastpresentandfuture.pdf). It is logical to assume, therefore, that if producers manage to manufacture cheaper units, and the ELT publishing industry produces interesting and stimulating software, the IWB stands a real chance of being the first modern technological teaching tool to bridge the gap between the 'technophiles' and the 'technophobes'. Although, as pointed out in Chapter 9, if training is poor, the introduction of this technology will not be a success.

But what else might we expect in the future? Any predictions made in a book like this one will undoubtedly be subject to revision over the next few years, but we hope that our suggestions and areas for further study will prove useful to you. One thing that is certain is that while the teaching profession may not be changing as quickly as we might have expected, technology is still moving on at an astounding place, and the software and hardware we use are gradually converging into devices which are more user-friendly and which integrate a myriad of services in one place.

Lastly, the pace of change will vary for different groups of teachers. Some groups will move very quickly to adopt new technologies and new habits while others will remain largely unaffected by technological changes. There will be no one big movement or trend, but rather a range of trends, some fast moving, others slow.

How to keep up-to-date

In Chapter 11 we covered various ways of interacting with other colleagues interested in the use of different technologies in the classroom, and looked at websites and online groups for continual development in this area. But accessing these different websites and joining these online groups does raise the issue of how to manage a potential deluge of information and ideas. Imagine that you regularly read five blogs related to teaching, and another three blogs related to using ICT in the language classroom, as well as two online journals which are published monthly. Calculate the amount of time you would spend every day going to all these sites to check on the latest postings. This is where **RSS**, or **Really Simply Syndication**, can make a huge difference to our everyday lives by helping us cope quickly and efficiently with the large amounts of new information produced daily.

RSS refers to a way of reading content from blogs and websites. How does this work? You install an RSS reader like Sharp Reader on your computer, or use an online reader like Bloglines, and every time you open the reader, it automatically goes along to all of the blogs and websites you are subscribed to, checks for new postings and articles, and downloads the headlines of these into your RSS reader, in a list format. You can then skim through these headlines to get an idea of recent postings or articles. To actually read any of the new content, you simply click on the headline, and you are taken to the story itself. RSS allows busy people to skim a large number of websites on a daily basis, quickly pinpointing interesting articles. It is, basically, a time-saver.

Web 2.0

The way we work with technology is undergoing a swift period of change, and the emphasis now is very much on the emergence of what has become known as Web 2.0, which perceives the transition of the World Wide Web from a disparate collection of websites to a fully-fledged computing platform, which delivers services and applications (software programs) to end users, wherever they may be. This is resulting in a vast collection of websites and services which are more social in nature, inviting people to share what they find, what they do and what they learn in a wide variety of contexts. You may read, for example, about **social bookmarking**, where people keep their bookmarks or favourites on a website instead of on their own computer. These bookmarks are tagged and described, and anyone also using the site can benefit from your collection of useful addresses – as you can from theirs.

A good example of a social bookmarking site is Del.Icio.Us (www.del.icio.us). In the screenshot below you will see a collection of teaching-related bookmarks shared by a colleague, Valentina Dodge. This bookmarking can save other teachers time by giving them the benefit of another user's experience and research. However, it must also be borne in mind that more access to this kind of information does not necessarily make life easier, having as it does the potential to overwhelm the user with information and sources of good material. One of the more important skills to be developed in the future will be that of sifting large quantities of information into useable chunks, and we will all need to develop faster information processing and evaluation skills if we are to make the most of this new platform, which is where software tools like RSS prove so useful.

We have looked at other social sites like wikis and blogs in the course of this book, and the list is growing. You can now find community-driven sites in many areas, from places where people share their music tastes and discover musicians recommended by other users, to collaborative online calendars and enormous collections of images and videos all uploaded, described and made available by the users themselves.

It has always been said that content is king, but what is interesting about this change is that the content is now not necessarily the domain of the bigger commercial companies, who are in a position to charge for what they supply, but is increasingly supplied by users for users. You only have to look at the number of public-produced videos and images making their way on to websites and news programmes to see how the model is changing.

MySpace, a social networking site primarily used by younger **Netizens** has recently been linked to the success of pop artists The Arctic Monkeys and Lily Allen, while other social sharing sites have been the launch pad for musicians such as Sandi Thorn, who attracted over 100,000 listeners to her concerts broadcast over the Internet. It is this long-hailed democratisation of content, and user-driven sites, which is marking the change in the way that the Internet delivers content.

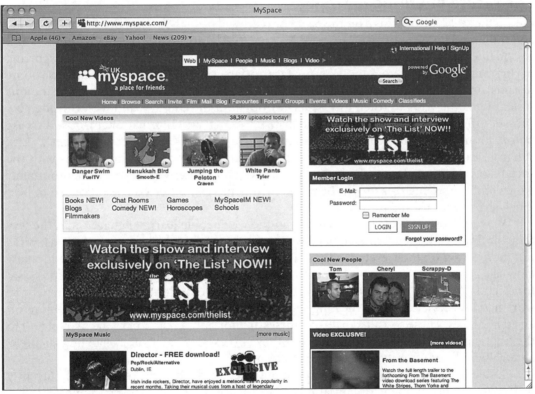

These sites would seem to have a part to play in language teaching. When the consumer also becomes the producer, shared knowledge and resources will take on a greater value, allowing teachers to pick and choose what they want to use in each class and promoting greater personalisation of the teaching and learning processes. In effect, the use of social websites should encourage a more eclectic approach to teaching, and it is to be hoped that the teaching experience will be further enhanced by the teacher's ability to provide tailored practice and personalised learning opportunities for each individual, without the effort this may have involved in the pre-digital age.

Not only will this shared approach enhance language teaching, but it will also have an impact on continuous professional development, with teachers creating their own personalised pages, drawing together blog feeds, video materials, essays and articles from a variety of sources into an ever-changing personal development site of their own. A site like this will constantly evolve and update to suit the teacher's developmental needs at any given point, and as such will be vastly different from more formal learning situations, and be based on 'just-in-time' solutions to particular training needs which involve a wider collection of people, all working towards shared goals. In effect, Web 2.0 may well become the biggest training institution in the world. You can find out more about Web 2.0 by looking it up in Wikipedia. If you want to investigate the kind of things which can be done in Web 2.0, you could start by looking at 'All Things Web 2.0' (http://www.sacredcowdung.com/archives/2006/03/all_things_web.html).

The future of online learning

One of the real growth areas over the next few years will be in the area of distributed learning and training. This is particularly relevant in contexts where the costs of a few computers and a good Internet connection are far lower than the more traditional approach of transporting participants and tutors to a location for face-to-face training. In the training area, some organisations, such as the Cultura Inglesa schools in Brazil, have already been using this system for some years to reach its teachers throughout the country, and with considerable success. Other organisations such as the British Council and International House also use online training solutions for teacher training via a virtual learning environment (VLE). What we expect to see happening is more online training, but combining VLEs with the social tools mentioned in the Web 2.0 section above and other virtual reality environments which add the feeling of actually 'being there' to what can otherwise be perceived to be a lonely experience for the trainee.

We would also expect to see a change in the way people learn languages, and the way they continue with their professional development or lifelong learning as time constraints put more strain on their everyday lives. This can already be seen on a small scale in many language centres around the world, with students no longer attending timetabled classes for a certain number of hours per week, but preferring to undertake a lot of the repetitive work in self-access mode, and meeting colleagues and a tutor for tutorial-based sessions on an ad hoc basis. These so-called hybrid courses are not only a reaction to the market and to the frantic pace of life of many people, but they also exist to cater for a changing clientele, a more 'wired' community – the Net generation.

Online learning will probably also mutate into a hybrid form of how it is currently delivered. At the moment organisations tend to use a VLE to deliver online learning, but these services can often be sterile in terms of providing the kind of communication opportunities we usually consider vital to the language learning process. It is highly likely that the more static material which can be offered in a VLE will be complemented by some of the social sites we mentioned above, and better synchronous tools such as peer-to-peer voice chat via Skype or similar software. This integration of services will allow for a more rounded user experience, and significantly improve the uptake in the area of language learning and teaching online.

It will also probably be the case that these will be combined with software that more actively encourages the development of communities of practice (see Chapter 11) to further enhance the social constructivist nature of the learning taking place there. These may be tools as simple as wikis and blogs, but may also be something along the lines of Elgg Learning Landscape (http://www.tesl-ej.org/ej34/m1.html) which is 'A Web publishing application combining the elements of weblogging, e-portfolios and social networking designed to promote learning through sharing of knowledge, conversation and reflection in a social/academic setting'.

Finding out more

A good place to get started would be to investigate VLEs (Virtual Learning Environments) which we have focused on already, and **Content Management Systems** (CMSs). A CMS is a web-based application that allows for the creation and management of information – you might like to think of it as a more structured kind of wiki. Essentially, it is an online repository which can be stocked with web pages, documents, downloads of multimedia files and other resources. It can be managed by a group of people, making it a useful collaborative environment in terms of pure information sharing. Basically, it makes the publishing of web pages easier and more structured. A good example of a CMS is Etomite (www.etomite.org). With excellent documentation and community support, it is a user-friendly entry point into the world of information management. Again, this can be freely downloaded, installed on a computer at home and experimented with. Etomite is relatively easy to install, and very easy to manage and use. A good use of such a system would be for a staff communication and training area, allowing users to add content, or for a staff reading group or working party investigating a facet of teaching.

You may well find that once you are used to using something like Etomite you will want to step up to a VLE, which allows not only for detailed information management, but which also enables structured online training and development, learner tracking, assessment and a host of other tools that will give you the opportunity to investigate the world of online teaching. One place to start would be to try out the free thirty-day trial offered by Blackboard (www.blackboard.com), as this will give you some idea of what you can achieve with a VLE and whether it is going to be a viable tool in your professional life. Should you find that a VLE is suited to the direction you wish to go in, however, you will either need to make a significant investment in Blackboard, or look to an open-source solution like Moodle.

Moodle is a free VLE, developed by a worldwide community. It is currently used by more than 56 percent of higher education establishments in the United Kingdom and has been adopted by the Open University in the United Kingdom, the largest distance education provider in the world. It is an ongoing creation, and will only continue to improve now that the Open University has given financial resources to improve its collection of services. You can try out Moodle on your home computer with a download (www.moodle.org), or look for a web hosting company who will install and run it for you on one of their servers. More information on such companies is available online (http://moodle.com/partners/list/).

A VLE allows you to create online courses and to enrol students in them. Inside the courses themselves you can combine various resources (pages of information and links to websites or files) with more interactive elements, like quizzes, questionnaires, structured lessons, forums and chat rooms, to make up the course content. We use Moodle for our online training courses, and it really is a flexible distance education package. Remember, however, that distance training and teaching is not the 'cheap' alternative that many people consider it to be. Indeed, development and tutoring costs for online courses can often surpass those for more traditional ones, so you would be wise to stop and consider why you might want to develop such courses, where your market lies and what skills you will need to acquire to implement them before going too far down the development path.

Virtual learning

'Virtual reality' is a term which has been around for so long with so few tangible results. And you may be led to thinking that it was a fanciful idea of the late twentieth century that never really caught on. Yet things have developed considerably in the past few years, and products are now starting to appear which make use of this 'other world' for training and education. You may see virtual reality environments referred to as MOOs (Multi-User Dimension Object Oriented) or simply as MUDs (Multi-User Dimension/Dungeon/ Dialogue). MOOs sprang up out of online gaming, hence the dungeon reference in the name. Basically, this means that they are networked environments which allow interaction between several people, and also interaction with virtual objects. You may also see them referred to as **MUVEs** (Multi-User Virtual Environments). For many years these were purely text-based places in which people text chatted and described objects and actions, but recent developments in computing and video speeds, as well as faster access to the Internet, have allowed for richer, graphically-based environments.

Finding out more

The most popular of the virtual reality worlds is currently **Second Life**. Set up by the former chief technical officer of Real Networks (the people who make Real Player), it is described on their website as 'a 3-D virtual world entirely built and owned by its residents'. Since opening to the public in 2003, it has grown explosively and today is inhabited by over three million people from around the globe. From the moment you enter the World you'll discover a vast digital continent, teeming with people, entertainment, experiences and opportunity. Once you've explored a bit, perhaps you'll find a perfect parcel of land to build your house or business. You'll also be surrounded by the creations of your fellow residents. Because residents retain the rights to their digital creations, they can buy, sell and trade with other residents' (http://secondlife.com/whatis/). To use Second Life you will need to download the program from the Second Life website and register for a username and password. At the time of writing this is free. You will also need to upgrade your Quicktime Player to the latest version (http://www.apple.com/quicktime/). Once you have done this, log in and start to explore. It is a strange virtual world peopled by the same curious mix as exists in real life, so don't be surprised if you see people fighting, flirting and doing all the other things you might expect to see outside in the street.

For educational purposes, Second Life provides an ideal and safe environment in which to work. Objects which react as they do in real life can be created, and in our research we came across plenty of training scenarios including Japanese classes, disaster relief training, first aid training and a heart murmur treatment simulation, among many others. While writing this chapter, we sat in on a variety of classes and courses in Second Life, and were constantly amazed by the degree of imagination used in combining real-life classes with 'in-world' (i.e. inside Second Life) sessions, including one course in Rhetoric and Composition being run by Sarah Robbins at Ball State University, Indiana, which meets once a week at the actual university, and once a week in Second Life. These innovative uses of new technologies give pause for thought, but also encourage us to look beyond our day-to-day practice to examine how we might incorporate them into what we do, where appropriate and desirable – a caveat we would encourage readers to keep uppermost in their minds when dealing with technology at any level. In Second Life there are also opportunities for more complex events such as seminars and conferences, as various combinations of media types are possible, from PowerPoint presentations, through audio and video streaming media, to various interaction types like quizzes, feedback forms and questionnaires.

A virtual seminar room in Second Life

At the time of writing it is expected that Second Life will soon have a version of the Firefox browser built into it. This will enable people in a room or public place to browse websites together, making it perfectly possible to build working terminals which would allow access to, for example, Moodle courses from within the world itself. There is also the suggestion that an audio client along the lines of Skype will also be incorporated. One project – Sloodle (www.sloodle.com) – is also looking at enabling Moodle to communicate with Second Life, and vice versa. It is this kind of innovation which may impact hugely on online training in the future, with the pedagogical rigour of a platform like Moodle linked closely to a social environment like Second Life providing a more lifelike and familiar learning space for many.

A world like this, with all its media possibilities, web browsing and audio has plenty of potential in all sorts of areas, and it will be the case that we will see more opportunities for language teaching and training inside these worlds as communications and graphics possibilities improve in coming years. Already a company called LanguageLab is planning to open a language school inside Second Life, and more are sure to follow. For more on education in Second Life, try the SimTeach website (www.simteach.com) or download and install Second Life and search for some of the groups that are exploring this emerging phenomenon, for example, Real Life Educators in Second Life, The Learning Society and the Educator's Coffee House. You'll find plenty of helpful people in these groups who will be able to get you started.

m-learning

m-learning is mobile learning and this includes the use of mobile phones, MP3 players, Personal Digital Assistants (PDAs) such as Palm hand-held computers and devices using Windows Mobile Computing platforms such as the iPAQ. While this may seem to be a bit of a fad, recent research has suggested that m-learning works well in environments where access to these kind of technologies is more normal and accepted or where lifestyles demand more flexible solutions to training and learning. A good example would be Japan, where it is not uncommon to see commuters on long train journeys use hand-held devices containing downloaded content to practise for the TOEIC test.

Finding out more

Agnes Kukulska-Hulme, a lecturer in educational technology at the Open University, is one of the principal practitioners in this field, using mobile technologies to deliver lecture notes and other key information via a myriad of portable technologies including smartphones and tablet PCs. With John Traxler she coedited the groundbreaking *Mobile Learning: A Handbook for Educators and Trainers*. This book features (among other articles) a study on a project aimed at teaching Italian via SMS (Short Message Service), written by Mike Levy. This is just one example of how teachers and technology are repositioning themselves to capitalise on the new literacy skills of the younger generation. You may also want to take a look at Kukulska-Hulme's case studies (http://iet.open.ac.uk/pp/a.m.kukulska-hulme/agnes.html).

There is a department of m-learning research at Birmingham University (UK) (http://www.mlearning.bham.ac.uk/). Here you can find out about their experiments with tablet PCs. Mobile CALL Projects, based in Nagoya, Japan, has an excellent website (http://www.studypatch.net/mobile/), where you can learn more about their projects with language learning and mobile platforms. For a short taster, here's what they say about a recent project: 'We emailed English vocabulary lessons at timed intervals to the mobile phones of 44 Japanese university students, hoping to promote regular study. Compared with students urged to regularly study identical materials on paper or web, students receiving mobile email learned more. 71% of the subjects preferred receiving these lessons on mobile phones rather than PCs. 93% felt this a valuable teaching method.'

One of the first ELT-related m-learning themed conferences was held by JALT CALL (Japanese Association of Language Teachers) in 2006, and you can find out more information about that online (http://jaltcall.org/news/). In short, m-learning appears to be here to stay, and it is – especially when we consider how adept most people are with mobile phones these days – a logical step forward in delivering 'content' to 'users' – or teaching, as it is sometimes called outside the world of technology! If all this seems a bit beyond your capabilities, try these two simple SMS-based activities with your learners and see how much interest is generated – it may just be the way in that you are looking for. The first activity does not use 'text speak' while the second is based entirely around this phenomenon.

Beginners m-learning activity

In this activity each member of the group needs to have a mobile phone. Each member writes down a list of class first names in alphabetical order. They then ask each other for their mobile phone numbers, noting down each one on their list. Once they have all the information, they send a simple SMS text question to the person on the list under their name with the last person on the list sending to the first. Each learner then reads the question they have received and replies to the sender. As a homework extension, each learner can send a different question to the person above them on the list.

This is a short example of introducing mobile technologies into the classroom, but it serves the purpose of showing learners what can be achieved with technology, and may also help them to improve their level of comfort with using mobile phones in the target language. It also opens up the possibility for more teacher-led m-learning activities like 'Word of the day', where you send them a vocabulary item to learn on a daily basis.

Advanced texting activity: '2b/-2b=?'*

If you're looking at the title of this activity and wondering what it means, here's a clue: it's a quotation from a Shakespeare play. While our backs were turned, a new kind of English emerged, texting (or txtng), which is now a main form of communication for millions of people around the globe. In this activity we look at how to exploit this phenomenon in the classroom and, no, you don't have to know how it all works, and it won't cost you a penny.

This all started with a composition handed in by a British schoolgirl after the summer break – a composition which she had written entirely as a text message. Her teacher was outraged (and bemused) and it wasn't long before the story appeared on the Internet. And this got us thinking about how we can help our learners to play with English using the technology that they are already familiar with.

The activity

Start off with a general warmer about mobile phones and texting, perhaps a questionnaire to be done individually and then discussed in pairs or small groups. This should be a popular topic with learners of all ages, so should generate a fair bit of discussion. Once this stage has been done, introduce the story of the British schoolgirl and then hand out the composition. Note that this is a fairly difficult text, with quite a few cultural references and other less tangible language, so you may want to edit it down into something more manageable for your learners.

> My smmr hols wr CWOT. B4, we usd 2go2 NY 2C my bro, his GF & thr 3 :- kds
> Bt my Ps wr so {:-/ BC o 9/11 tht they dcdd 2 stay in SCO & spnd 2wks up N.
> Up N, WUCIWUG -- o. I ws vvv brd in MON. o bt baas & ^^^^^. AAR8, my Ps
> wr :-) -- they sd ICBW, & tht they wr ha-p 4 the pc&qt...IDTS!! I wntd 2 go hm
> ASAP, 2C my M8s again. 2day, I cam bk 2 skool. I feel v O:-) BC I hv dn all my
> hm wrk. Now its BAU...

Draw the following grid on the board and get learners to copy it and fill it in with whatever they can understand from the composition:

---

* 2b/-2b=? 'To be, or not to be? That is the question.' (Shakespeare's *Hamlet*)

English text	English word	Word in your language	Text in your language
B4	Before		

They should be able to understand a fair bit and this is a great opportunity to allow your learners to teach you a little bit about their world (and their language) in the feedback phase when the table is filled in collaboratively.

Follow-ups

There are plenty of possible follow-ups. You may want to try a rewrite activity in which learners produce a short text in 'texting language' and then rewrite it 'properly'. Or try having your learners engage in 'texting' conversations using Post-It notes on the class wall. Lastly, you could send your students a daily phrase or word to learn in 'texting' language.

Composition key

> My summer holidays were a complete waste of time. Before, we used to go to New York to see my brother, his girlfriend and their three screaming kids face-to-face. I love New York, it's a great place. But my parents were so worried because of the terrorism attack on September 11 that they decided we would stay in Scotland and spend two weeks up north. Up north, what you see is what you get – nothing. I was extremely bored in the middle of nowhere. Nothing but sheep and mountains. At any rate, my parents were happy. They said that it could be worse, and that they were happy with the peace and quiet. I don't think so! I wanted to go home as soon as possible, to see my mates again. Today I came back to school. I feel very saintly because I have done all my homework. Now it's business as usual...

Whatever you experiment with, be it online, virtual or mobile, you must ensure that equal access is available to all of your students, and that your teaching and your students' learning is enhanced by the chosen approach. It is far too easy to be impressed by the technology, to the point of forgetting that perhaps a more traditional approach might work better. We offer these insights only as pointers as to where education may be going and to areas you may consider exploring in your own teaching.

Conclusions | *In this chapter we have:*

- looked at the concept of Web 2.0.
- considered where the Internet is heading in the future.
- explored the future of online learning.
- considered the application of virtual learning.
- examined m-learning and seen two basic activities to introduce it into your teaching.

> ON THE CD-ROM YOU CAN HEAR TWO TEACHERS TALKING ABOUT HOW THEY SEE THE FUTURE, WATCH A TUTORIAL ON USING RSS AND HAVE A LOOK AT SECOND LIFE.

Introduction

- The activities in this section all relate to topics discussed in the chapter to which the exercises refer.
- Most activities have page references to point you towards the relevant part of the chapter. However, some activities require you to read through the whole chapter, so have no specific references.
- Some questions asked here expect definite answers, while others ask only for your ideas and opinions.
- Tutors can decide when it is appropriate to use the tasks in this section. Readers on their own can work on the tasks at any stage in their reading of the book.
- An answer key is provided after the Task File (on pages 175–182) for those tasks where it is possible to provide specific or suggested answers. The symbol ✔ beside an exercise indicates that answers are given for that exercise.
- The material in the Task File can be photocopied for use in limited circumstances. Please see the note on page 2 for photocopying restrictions.

Chapter 1: Technology in the classroom

A Technophobe or technogeek? Or somewhere in between?
(pages 8–11)

How do you feel about technology? Do this 'Attitudes to technology' questionnaire and then read the commentary in the answer key.

1 = disagree totally 2 = disagree 3 = no strong opinion 4 = agree 5 = agree strongly

Attitudes to technology	1	2	3	4	5
1 I enjoy using technology.					
2 I avoid using technology when I can.					
3 I think using technology in class takes up too much time.					
4 I know that technology can help me to learn many new things.					
5 Technology intimidates and threatens me.					
6 Teachers should know how to use technology in class.					
7 I would be a better teacher if I knew how to use technology properly.					
8 I'm very confident when it comes to working with technology in class.					
9 I want to learn more about using technology in class.					
10 I believe that the Internet can really improve my teaching practice.					
11 Changing the curriculum to integrate technology is impossible.					
12 Technology breaks down too often to be of very much use.					

B Why should teachers use technology?

On a piece of paper or below, make a list of good reasons for using technology in your professional life and in your classroom teaching practice. Think about presentation, methodology, approaches, task variety, motivation and specific ICT tools.

- *more attractive teaching materials*
-
-
-
-

Chapter 2: Word processors in the classroom

A Using word processors 🔑

List six good reasons for using word processors in the classroom.

1 ....
2 ....
3 ....
4 ....
5 ....
6 ....

Now note down three potential problems learners may have.

7 ....
8 ....
9 ....

B Word processing skills questionnaire 🔑

Assess your own word processing skills. What do you know?

I can ...	Yes	No
... open, save, retrieve and print documents.		
... select text using the keyboard.		
... select text using the mouse.		
... cut, copy and paste.		
... drag and drop.		
... search and replace.		
... use TrackChanges.		
... use forms.		

Which of these skills do you think your learners would need? Redesign the questionnaire so that you can use it as a diagnostic test with your classes.

C Word processing skills – learner training 🔑

In which order would you cover these skills with your learners?

- Search and replace
- Opening, saving, retrieving and printing documents
- TrackChanges
- Undo and redo changes made
- Dragging and dropping
- Cutting, copying and pasting
- Selecting text (mouse and keyboard)

Chapter 3: Using websites

A Finding useful websites – search techniques (pages 29–34)

1 You want your learners to plan a weekend trip in London. Which of the following phrases would yield the best results in a keyword search engine such as Google?

a things to do in London.

b plan a weekend in London.

c weekend trip in London.

2 A subject guide such as Yahoo! has some of the following categories:

a Arts	**e** Government	**i** Reference
b Business	**f** Health	**j** Regional
c Education	**g** News & Media	**k** Science
d Entertainment	**h** Recreation & Sports	

In which category would you search for the following information?

1 a phone number in New York ☐

2 the latest Pulitzer prize winner for music ☐

3 basic first aid procedures for choking ☐

4 intellectual copyright law ☐

5 space exploration on Mars ☐

6 a movie review of *Lord of the Rings* ☐

7 the capital of Andorra ☐

8 online Dutch language courses ☐

9 a BBC Radio 4 programme ☐

10 the head of the World Trade Organisation ☐

11 cooking tips for asparagus ☐

3 A real language search engine such as Ask uses real questions. Which of the searches in Activity 2 above can be turned into real questions, and what are the questions?

B Evaluating websites (pages 34–35)

Look at the Guinness World Records website (http://www.guinnessworldrecords.com/) and evaluate it according to the following criteria:

- accuracy (content and linguistic accuracy)
- currency
- content
- functionality

C Planning lessons using the Internet (pages 36–39)

Look at the newsmap website and the lesson plan. Match the stages – warmer, web, what next – to the descriptions.

The news is an upper-intermediate to advanced lesson concentrating on current news. The class uses the newsmap website (http://www.marumushi.com/apps/newsmap/newsmap.cfm).

Stage	Description
	Learners come together as a class to produce a news programme for the day. This can also be videoed or audio recorded if the necessary equipment is available.
	What are the main news stories of the day? Get learners into four groups to brainstorm stories in each of the following categories (one per group): world, national, sports, entertainment. Have them mind-map the stories in their category on the board and explain what is happening in their category.
	In small groups, learners choose one of the stories from a newsmap category and research it further. They make notes as they find out more details.

D Web teaching dos and don'ts

You are giving a new teacher advice about using the Internet in their classes. Which of the following pieces of advice would you give, and which would you not? Why?

1	Use websites that will probably be new for your learners.	
2	Lesson planning for using a website is very different from planning using a coursebook.	
3	It's best to use websites that have lots of movement and flashing lights and sound, to keep learners interested.	
4	It's a good idea to have a backup plan in case of problems with the technology.	
5	Don't let your learners know that you're not confident with the technology. They might lose respect for you.	
6	To use a web page you don't have to have a live Internet connection. You can download and save a website to your computer before the class, or you can print a website out.	
7	Learners should work alone on the computer, not in pairs or groups.	
8	Keep the learners in front of the computers for the whole class if possible, even for work which does not need them looking at the screen. Moving them is disruptive.	

A Internet-based project work (pages 44–53) 🔑

Choose one of the following project work ideas. Use your search skills to find three suitable websites for learners to research your chosen topic.

a A project for young learners aged 12–13 on Ancient Egypt.
Level of English: elementary (upper primary).
Outcome: learners need to produce a poster in small groups showing two or three aspects of daily life in Ancient Egypt.

b A project for adult learners of general English on extreme sports.
Level of English: low intermediate.
Outcome: in pairs or small groups, learners need to present an example of one extreme sport to the class, either on a poster or using PowerPoint.

c A project for adult learners of business English on Benetton's advertising campaigns and the creation of a brand image.
Level of English: advanced.
Outcome: learners need to design and present a new billboard advertisement for Benetton, justifying how it fits in with Benetton's brand image.

B Structure of webquests (pages 54–57) 🔑

A good webquest usually contains four stages: Introduction – Task – Process – Evaluation. Look at the sample webquest and match the stages to the correct sentence.

Off to Oz – A trip to Australia	
Stage	**Description**
	Learners are given the job of finding out about Australia ahead of planning a trip there.
	Learners reflect on what they have done and how they contributed to the overall process.
	Learners investigate various web-based resources on Australia, making a quiz for their colleagues, preparing an interview on their experiences and making a travel brochure based on their findings.
	Learners discuss the idea of visiting an English-speaking country – the similarities and differences, possible likes and dislikes, things they would miss, things they would take with them.

A full version of this webquest can be found online (http://www.xtec.es/crle/02/webquests/english/3index2.html).

C Using webquests with your learners (pages 54–57) 🔑

Look at the descriptions of the following webquests from an online repository. For each webquest, consider:

- What level of learners would this be suitable for (beginner, low/high intermediate, advanced)?
- What age would this be most suitable for (young learners, adolescents, adults)?
- What language context would this be most suitable for (general English, business English, teacher training, English for peacekeeping purposes, etc)?

a Carnival crime

In this webquest, students are police officers working for Interpol, and investigate a crime committed during the Carnival in Rio, Brazil. Students examine Interpol's most wanted criminals list, communicate with other 'police', and find a suspect for the crime, presenting their findings to a police commission.

b The TESOL methodology webquest

This webquest explores in a fun way the history, methods, approaches and applications of English Language Teaching. You'll meet many of the 'big names', encounter some exotic methods and techniques, and learn a lot about your own teaching in the process.

c The Top 10

This webquest is based on current pop music. The students compare the current 'Top 10' in their own country, in the UK and in the US.

d Computer games

In this webquest students find out about computer games and the people who play them. They will be asked how they feel about computer games, and will use the web to read what other people think.

e Christmas

This webquest is a project for a student-produced magazine on the theme of Christmas. Students research a range of Christmas-related topics, such as Christmas through history and Christmas traditions, and they produce contributions for a class magazine.

f A trip to an English-speaking city

London, Toronto, New York, Sydney, Cape Town and many more – all large, vibrant, multicultural cities, rich in history and with many beautiful and interesting places to visit. The purpose of this webquest is to plan a visit to one of the cities, where you will stay for one month studying English at a language school and, above all, having fun!

Which of these webquests would you use with your learners? Try them out!

A Questionnaire on your use of email (pages 62–70)

How ready are you as a teacher to use email with your learners? Try this questionnaire.

Email questionnaire – How much do you know about the following?	A lot	A bit	Nothing
1 The benefits of using email with learners.			
2 Setting up an email account in Yahoo! or Hotmail.			
3 Email viruses.			
4 Setting spam filters on email.			
5 Finding out about your learners' email skills.			
6 Sending and opening email attachments.			
7 The 'text-speak' conventions used in email.			
8 Using email with your learners out of class.			
9 Classroom-based email projects such as data collection projects or keypal projects.			
10 The issues involved in setting up a keypal project.			

B Email: genre and appropriacy (pages 62–63)

Look at the following email written to solicit information from the website 'Save the Whale'. Circle the elements that are inappropriate, and note down why they are inappropriate. Then rewrite the email in a more appropriate style.

> Hi! I LIKE YOUR SITE 'Save the Whale'.
> im preparing for a presentation at my school about why whales are in danger of extinction ☺
> i want u to send me some stuff about this, like brochures, posters etc!!!!! i need it by tonite!!!!!!
> CU!

C Using email: issues (pages 62–70)

Below is a series of issues that might arise when using email with learners. Suggest a solution for each.

    a Your learners don't have email accounts.

    b Your learners don't know how to send or open email attachments.

    c Your learners use abbreviations such as *CU* ('see you') or the lower case *i* in all their emails.

    d You would like to provide your learners with a weekly emailed summary of classwork covered, but have no time to do so.

    e Your learners are reluctant to do the extra work that belonging to a class email discussion list involves, and do not contribute much.

    f In a keypal project, your learners don't know what to write to their partner in another country.

    g Your learners are upset by emails received from the partner country, as they find them 'rude' or 'aggressive'.

Chapter 6: How to use chat

A Using chat in language teaching (pages 71–84)

Do you agree or disagree with the following statements? Why?

   a With text chat, we need to teach learners to use 'text speak', e.g. *L8er* for 'later'.

   b Voice chat is easier to use than text chat.

   c The teacher requires a lot of technical knowledge to use text or voice chat with learners.

   d It's a good idea to teach learners some chat conventions, e.g. how to take turns.

   e Using chat is best between classes who already meet regularly face-to-face.

B Chat activities with learners (pages 74–84)

Look at the following chat activities. Which activities would work better with text chat, which would work better with voice chat, and which could work well with either text or voice chat?

	Text	Voice	Either
1 A group of learners, who usually meet face-to-face, use chat outside class to discuss a summary of project work, which they will need to present to the class.			
2 A group of learners in Italy interview a group of learners in India to find out about the most important religious festival of the year in the two countries.			
3 A group of Spanish learners (learning English in Spain) chat with a group of English-speakers in Canada (who are learning Spanish), to practise the pronunciation of certain Spanish and English words.			
4 Two secondary school classes chat in pairs about their favourite music and groups.			
5 Learners in the same class chat in pairs to practise 'text speak' conventions, such as *btw* ('by the way').			
6 The teacher is available via chat on Wednesday evenings from 7–8 p.m. (outside teaching hours) to answer any questions about homework or assignments, or to chat to learners about anything they like.			

C Types of chat (pages 71–73)

1 Match the type of chat with the correct definition.

   a free topic chat   **1** a chat in which one participant gives information on a topic

   b task-oriented chat   **2** a chat which requires learners to produce an outcome or 'product'

   c informative chat   **3** a chat which provides opportunities to practise a specific function

   d practice chat   **4** a chat which has no pre-set theme to discuss, or one clear moderator

2 Look again at the chat activities suggested in Activity B above. For each, decide whether it is an example of a free topic chat, a task-oriented chat, an informative chat or a practice chat.

Chapter 7: Blogs, wikis and podcasts

A Terminology: blogs, wikis and podcasts (pages 86–102) ☞

Match the terminology to the definition.

1 social software		**a**	The lack of enthusiasm one feels for one's blog, after a time.
2 blogroll		**b**	A well-known collaborative encyclopedia on the Internet.
3 edublog		**c**	An audio or video file which can be downloaded to a personal computer or to a mobile device such as an MP3 player.
4 blogfade		**d**	ICT tools which encourage users to collaborate and communicate online. Typically they allow multiple authorship, and content is generated by the users.
5 Blogger.com		**e**	A collaborative webspace consisting of several linked web pages, that can be edited by several people.
6 vlog		**f**	A blog used in education.
7 wiki		**g**	A video blog.
8 Wikipedia		**h**	A user-friendly site where one can easily create and record a podcast.
9 pbwiki		**i**	A podcast in the form of a video.
10 podcast		**j**	The software needed to download a podcast.
11 podcatching software		**k**	Course lectures delivered in podcast format – increasingly popular in tertiary education.
12 Vodcast		**l**	A list of links to other blogs.
13 coursecasting		**m**	A well-known site where one can easily set up a blog.
14 podOmatic		**n**	A user-friendly site where one can easily set up a wiki.

B Blogs (pages 87–90) ☞

What kind of blog would be most suitable for the following activities: a tutor blog (T), a student blog (S) or a class blog (C)?

1 a blog with personal information, such as hobbies and interests, family or home. ☐
2 a blog with links to further explore topics covered in a speaking class. ☐
3 a blog setting extra homework activities for learners. ☐
4 a blog of class project work (posters produced, texts written, photographs). ☐
5 a blog describing learners' summer holidays. ☐
6 a blog describing different festival days in the learners' country/countries. ☐

C Wikis (pages 93–98) ☞

1 What is the essential difference between a blog and a wiki?
2 Which of the activities described in Activity B above could also work well in a wiki?

D Podcasts (pages 98–102) ☞

What are the advantages and disadvantages of listening to/creating podcasts?

	Advantages	Disadvantages
Learners listen to podcasts		
Learners create podcasts		

Chapter 8: Online reference tools

A Concordancers and corpuses – pros and cons
(pages 105–110)

Which of these do you think are good reasons for using concordancers and corpuses, and which are potential disadvantages?

1 They give access to a wide range of authentic English from native speakers.
2 They show a variety of 'Englishes', challenging the 'standard' English concept.
3 The data they return is culturally and contextually limited.
4 They encourage inductive approaches to grammar teaching/learning.
5 They cater to analytical learners.
6 They suggest that native speaker language models are better.
7 They clearly demonstrate differences between written and spoken English.

B The right tool (pages 103–112)

Which of these online tools would you recommend for the cases listed below?

thesaurus   translator   dictionary   encyclopedia   concordancer

1 A business English student who has to skim-read a lot of documents in English, but who does not quite have the level to do this comfortably.
2 A group of learners preparing for an exam who do not have a sufficient range of vocabulary for the written paper and always use the same few phrases repeatedly.
3 A lower-intermediate learner who has trouble remembering the pronunciation of certain words.
4 A proficiency-level learner who struggles with collocations and small vocabulary points.
5 A group of younger learners who are quite proficient in English, but lack any real experience in the world and are held back by this in many of the creative activities you plan.

Chapter 9: Technology-based courseware

A CD-ROMs (pages 113–114)

What skills and activity types are usually included on self-study CD-ROMs? Fill in the text below with these words and phrases.

> authentic   reorder sentences   listening   Free writing   writing   speaking   multiple choice

> Self-study CD-ROMs usually include activities to practise all four skills: the receptive skills – reading and (1) .... – and the productive skills – speaking and (2) .... Graded or (3) .... texts can be provided for both listening and reading activities, and comprehension tasks, such as matching or (4) .... , supplied. The writing skill is less easy to provide practice for on a CD-ROM, and activity types are often mechanical, requiring learners to (5) .... or words, or to fill in blanks in a paragraph. (6) .... activities need to be corrected by a teacher, so are often not included on a CD-ROM. The (7) .... skill is probably the most difficult to deal with effectively on a CD-ROM, and activities involving voice-recognition software are often flawed.

B Technology-based courseware: advantages and disadvantages (pages 113–119; 122–124)

Match one advantage and one disadvantage to each piece of courseware.

- Reliability in marking is high.
- Costs are high for the average teacher/school.
- Encourages autonomous learning.
- Speaking and writing are difficult to assess reliably.
- Materials in this medium look very impressive.
- Voice recognition software can be unreliable.

Courseware	Advantage	Disadvantage
CD-ROMs		
Computer-based testing		
Interactive whiteboards		

Chapter 10: Producing electronic materials

A Which Potato? (pages 129–132)

Can you match the Hot Potato tool to a description?

a JCloze	**1** This tool makes jumbled word activities.
b JMatch	**2** Make interactive word puzzles with clues.
c JQuiz	**3** Combine sets of exercises into websites.
d JCross	**4** Create to connect words with pictures, etc.
e JMix	**5** Use this one to make gap-fill exercises.
f The Masher	**6** Create short answer tests and games.

Note that the names of all the Hot Potato tools start with 'J'.

B In a Quandary (pages 132–135)

Put these steps for making a simple two-choice reading maze into the correct order. The first one is done for you.

- **a** Change to view Decision Point 2, and write the content.
- **b** Add a title to Decision Point 1.
- **c** Create a new maze. (1)
- **d** Save your maze.
- **e** Create a link to a new Decision Point (Decision Point 2).
- **f** Give your reading maze a title.
- **g** Change to view Decision Point 3, and write the content.
- **h** Export your reading maze to XHTML (make it into a web page).
- **i** Describe the basic situation in Decision Point 1, giving two options to choose from.
- **j** Create a link to a new Decision Point (Decision Point 3).

Chapter 11: e-learning: online teaching and training

A Online learning (pages 136–140)

Which of the following scenarios involve genuine 'online learning'?

1 Learners use an interactive CD-ROM at home to do extra language work.
2 Learners use a voice chat program like Skype once a month to chat with a class in another country.
3 Learners do 25 percent of classwork face-to-face, and 75 percent in the VLE (Virtual Learning Environment) Moodle.
4 A teacher does a one-month course on designing webquests entirely online, with a group of other teachers from around the world.
5 A teacher takes their class once a week to the computer lab, where learners use the Internet to research project work.
6 Learners are involved in an email exchange project with learners in another country.

B Online courses (pages 138–143)

What are some of the advantages and disadvantages of taking a 100 percent online language course from the learner's perspective?

Advantages	Disadvantages

C Communities of practice (pages 145–146) 🎸

Look at the posting below from a teacher who belongs to a distributed CoP. Which of the elements of a CoP can you identify in her posting? Match the underlined phrases in her posting with the CoP characteristics.

	Messages	Messages Help
Home		
Messages	Message # [ ] [Go] Search: [_____] [Search] Advanced	

Members Only
Post
Files
Photos
Database
Polls
Members
Calendar

Reply | Forward   < Prev Message | Next Message >

Dear Colleagues,

As you know, <u>I recently joined the group</u> as I'd heard about the great work you're all doing with <u>using ICT tools with your students</u>. I followed the discussion <u>led by Danny G</u> on setting up blogs with our students -- and the great news is that we've done it! My intermediate class now has <u>a class blog at www.classblog.blogspot.com</u> in which we describe some of the local festivals we have here in Italy.

It would be fantastic if some of you could get your students to come along and post some comments on our blog -- <u>I realise now I should have asked you all if you could come and post to our blog before we started</u> -- the students would have been even more motivated if they knew that students from other countries were going to visit the blog and read their work! Never mind, live and learn.

Paula

voluntary membership

an artefact

reflection on practice

a negotiated goal

a core member

🟢 Already a member? Sign in to Yahoo!

Yahoo! Groups Tips
Did you know...
Real people. Real stories. See how Yahoo! Groups impacts members worldwide.

🟢 Internet

start | 3 Compu... | WordPerfe... | Quattro Pr... | "Let It Be"... | 1637 | Microsoft ... | LearningTe... | EN | 16:04

Chapter 12: Preparing for the future

A Web 2.0 (pages 150–152)

Visit these 2.0 websites and find out what they offer.

a	www.flickr.com	shared wisdom
b	www.pandora.com	image repository
c	www.30boxes.com	project management
d	www.youtube.com	large file transfers
e	www.yousendit.com	online calendar
f	www.blinkbits.com	media bank
g	www.43things.com	news portal
h	www.zohoplanner.com	shared desktops
i	www.gabbr.com	life goals collection
j	www.centraldesktop.com	music management

B Future trends

Look at the different scenarios below and decide which tool would be best for the job:

mobile phones   a Virtual Learning Environment   a Content Management System
MP3 players   Second Life

a a busy director of studies who wants to set up new channels of communication with her teachers, to keep them up-to-date and to allow them to make suggestions.

b a teacher with little interest in traditional classes who works in a high-tech school with good technological facilities and programmers experienced in multimedia and games design.

c a teacher who is running a hybrid course (some self-study and some tutorials) who notices that his students have very little time to attend the tutorials and are missing out on useful information and explanations from these sessions.

d a teacher working with business English students who have very little time to study due to work pressures, but need constant help with expressing themselves in certain situations.

e a trainer working with groups of trainee teachers distributed over a wide geographical area.

C Keeping up with future trends

What have you learnt about future trends and tools in teaching with technology? Which of these things would you like to incorporate into your teaching and professional development?

Tool/Trend	I know what this is	I'd like to explore this more
RSS feeds		
Social bookmarking		
Use of a VLE (e.g. Moodle) or CMS (e.g. Etomite)		
Use of a MUVE (e.g. Second Life)		
m-learning (e.g. develop a podcast for learners)		
Use a mobile phone texting activity in class		
Join an online teacher development group		

TASK FILE KEY

Chapter 1

A

If you've chosen mostly 4s and 5s in questions 1, 4, 6, 7, 8, 9 and 10, then you have a very positive attitude to technology and are keen to learn more. If you have chosen mostly 4s and 5s in questions 2, 3, 5, 11 and 12, then perhaps you don't yet feel confident enough to use technology to its full potential.

A large part of the negative attitudes we have looked at in this first chapter are the result of a lack of confidence, a lack of facilities or a lack of training, resulting in an inability to see the benefit of using technologies in the classroom.

This book aims to help you build your confidence and increase your experience in using technology and to help you to see ways in which your teaching practice can be enhanced by it, even if you are teaching in a 'resource-poor' environment.

B

Here is a suggested list of good reasons to use ICT with learners.

1 Teachers can produce more attractive teaching materials.
2 It uses media which learners use in their daily life.
3 As an international language, English is increasingly being used in computer-mediated contexts, and using ICT with learners in class gives them practice for real-life ICT contexts.
4 Access to up-to-date materials via the Internet.
5 A change from using paper and pen, books and the board.
6 Adds variety to a lesson.
7 Keeps the teacher learning new skills.
8 May teach the learners new skills.
9 New ICT skills learnt in the classroom (e.g. Internet search skills) can be transferred to real life.
10 Makes the teacher look more professional.
11 Makes the school look more professional and up-to-date.
12 Learners can access authentic websites, as well as websites for EFL/ESL learners.
13 Some ICT tools (e.g. blogs, chat, email) can enable learners to make contact with learners in other countries.
14 Some ICT tools (e.g. online reference tools, CD-ROMs) can encourage learners to work alone, and can provide personalised feedback and assessment.
15 ICT tools can be used both in and outside the classroom.
16 The Internet can give teachers access to online teacher development groups and online training courses.
17 Using a range of ICT tools can give learners exposure to and practice in all of the four main language skills – speaking, listening, writing and reading.

Chapter 2

A

Suggested answer:

1 easy editing and correcting without rewriting.
2 encourages learners to take pride in their work.
3 activates noticing skills.
4 encourages learners to play with the language.

5 teaches basic ICT skills.
6 facilitates peer and teacher correction.
7 lack of basic computer skills.
8 lack of document handling skills.
9 over-reliance on grammar or spell-checker.

B

Suggested answer:

The last skill (using forms) is probably not needed by learners for classes involving the use of word processors. All the other skills will be useful for the activities in this chapter and in word processing classes in general.

C

Suggested answer:

The most logical thing would be to start with the document management skills such as opening, saving, retrieving and printing documents as these are basic skills on which the others will build. Then move on to selecting text, dragging and dropping it and cutting, copying and pasting. Then examine how to undo and redo actions. In the next stage you can introduce search and replace features and TrackChanges.

Chapter 3

A

1 **a** gives good results for official and general sights connected to London attractions, sightseeing, etc.

   b doesn't provide very good results apart from one prepared by schoolchildren which would be easier to use at lower levels.

   c leads to a lot of travel companies.

   On balance, **a** is probably the best search option.

2 **1** i **2** a **3** f **4** b **5** k **6** d **7** j **8** c **9** g **10** e **11** h

3

Suggested answers:

   2 Who won the Pulitzer prize for music in [year]?

   3 What should I do if someone chokes? What are the first aid procedures for choking?

   6 What do the reviews say about *Lord of the Rings*?

   7 What is the capital of Andorra?

   8 Where/How can I learn Dutch online?

   10 Who is the head of the World Trade Organisation?

   11 How can I cook asparagus?

Note that numbers 1, 4, 5 and 9 are too broad to formulate into specific questions.

B

Accuracy:

All of the information is verified by the Guinness team. The 'About us' section suggests a personal involvement in production by well-qualified people. Among other languages, the site can be browsed in British English, American English and Australian English, making it ideal for many different contexts. Linguistically accurate, with very little use of slang – short chunks suggest it might be very exploitable.

Currency:

Up-to-date with all the latest world records, the site seems to be updated every day (see the last updated information on the opening page). This is also suggested by the scrolling ticker with the latest records.

Content:

An excellent mix of short texts for each record is complemented by different sections (natural world, modern society, etc) and an interesting repository of video materials, games and a dedicated kids section.

Functionality:

The site works perfectly overall, though a couple of the games pages give script errors. It's also worth noting that additional software is necessary to play the games and to watch the videos. These will also need a faster connection for full enjoyment.

C

what next – warmer – web

D

Commentary:

1 New websites may well be more motivating for your learners, but it's worth bearing in mind that they may have their own favourite websites which you may be able to exploit in class, too.

2 This isn't usually the case. When we work with coursebooks we are working with someone else's material, and this is also true of using web pages. The main difference will be that websites are generally not prepared with the language learner in mind.

3 Visually attractive websites can be more interesting for learners, but you must also bear in mind that they are more likely to experience technical problems or be slow to load on slower connections.

4 As with all lesson ideas, a backup plan is vital. It's perhaps slightly more necessary when working with technology as there is a potentially higher chance of something going wrong at the last minute.

5 A class full of learners can really help take the pressure off the teacher with regard to technology. Ensure that your learners know what you are doing with regard to exploiting technology on a pedagogical level, but don't be afraid to use their experience. This also gives the learners a stake in the successful outcome of a technology-led class.

6 Both of these options are open to you. For smaller websites and the use of one-off pages this can be an ideal option. Don't forget, however, that using the Internet 'live' gives the whole lesson more immediacy and relevance.

7 It will obviously depend on the tasks, but having learners in pairs when using computers will encourage cooperation and hopefully lead to more language production throughout the process.

8 It's usually a good idea to have learners in front of the computers only when they are needed, and to move them away to a more 'communicative' and 'cooperative' work environment at other times. Moving learners can be positive for the class dynamic if handled properly.

Chapter 4

A

Websites chosen here should include the following features for each project:

Project **a**: Lots of visuals (drawings) illustrating daily life in Ancient Egypt, with very little text. Learners should be able to deduce elements of daily life from the pictures, not necessarily from reading the accompanying texts. A good example is (http://www.historyforkids.org/learn/egypt/index.htm).

Project **b**: Websites chosen here might include one site with various extreme sports, plus several sites for specific sports. Again, visuals on the sites chosen are important. An example might be (http://www.extreme.com/).

Project **c**: Obviously a site with a repository of past Benetton advertising posters is important, but the teacher might also want to provide a site which looks at successful billboard advertising. Example sites are (http://www.museedelapub.org/pubgb/virt/mp/benetton/pub_benetton.html) for Benetton posters and (http://www.communitystorage.com/outdoor/tips.htm) for a site on advertising.

Note: Some of the Benetton posters have been heavily criticised for their polemical and shocking content. You may want to check your chosen sites beforehand to ensure they are suitable for your learners.

B

Stages: Task – Evaluation – Process – Introduction

C

Suggested answers:

a Carnival crime: Suitable for intermediate and higher-level adults; general English and English for peacekeeping purposes.

b The TESOL methodology webquest: Suitable for higher-level adult trainees on teacher training courses.

c The Top 10: Suitable for lower-level adolescents; general English.

d Computer games: Suitable for intermediate older adolescents and adults; general English.

e Christmas: Suitable for younger learners, intermediate levels; general English.

f A trip to an English-speaking city: Suitable for adolescent and adult learners of general English, of low intermediate level or higher.

Chapter 5

B

Commentary:

The email uses the following 'text speak' forms, which are inappropriate for a semi-formal email asking for information:

- use of lower case *i* instead of *I*.
- misspellings – *im, tonite.*
- abbreviations – *u, CU.*
- overuse of punctuation (*!!!*) and inappropriate use of an emoticon (☺).

One sentence is written in upper case (*I LIKE YOUR SITE*), which is always inappropriate for email, as it comes across as 'shouting'.

The email should begin by addressing the reader. *Hi* (or *Hello*) is acceptable in a more 'formal' email if balanced with something more formal at the end like *Regards* or similar, and the writer's name.

It needs to include more general information such as who the writer is, what the school is and what the project is about.

C

Commentary:

Possible ways of solving the issues are as follows – note that these are just suggestions, and you may have thought of other, equally effective ways of dealing with the problems.

a Help your learners to set up email accounts with a free web-based email service such as Yahoo! or Hotmail.

b Provide your learners with some basic hands-on technical training in email use. This may or may not include covering areas such as virus protection or spam, depending on how much skill they already have.

c Make your learners aware of issues of appropriacy and netiquette in email use. You could use Task B above to do this.

d Encourage different learners to do this every week, and award credit for it, or make it part of a portfolio assessment.

e Be prepared to drop an idea if learners are not convinced of its value. If out-of-class email activities do not work, try an in-class email project such as a short information gathering activity, and be sure to discuss the benefits of such an activity with learners.

f Provide a clear task with detailed guidelines on what learners could write. This could take the form of a series of bullet points or questions. For lower-level learners, you could even provide a model email for learners to base their own emails on.

g Discuss issue of intercultural communication with your learners, and how their own first language norms in writing compare with English. What are the differences and similarities? How might this affect the partner country's writing of emails? It's a good idea to raise this issue in intercultural projects early on, so that learners are prepared for – and more tolerant of – differences in style and register.

Chapter 6
A

Commentary:

a It may be useful to teach your learners certain common abbreviations used in text chat like *CU* for 'see you' or *btw* for 'by the way', but you need to consider whether your learners really need to use text chat as native speakers do, or whether they will be using chat to contact other non-native speakers. Even if they do use chat to contact native speakers, do they need to sound like native speakers? In our opinion, using standard English in text chat is preferable, but this is also an issue worth discussing with your learners to see what they think.

b In terms of technical requirements, text chat may be easier to use than voice chat, as text chat requires less bandwidth, no sound card, microphone, speakers or headset. On the other hand, text chat can be slow, and weaker typists are put at a disadvantage. Also, in the single computer classroom, larger groups can take part simultaneously in voice chat more easily than in text chat, so which one is 'easier' to use with learners depends very much on your teaching context.

c Chat software is generally very easy to install and use. Although more complex chat software like Elluminate might require some initial training, less complex programs, like instant messaging, are very user-friendly and require no technical knowledge to install and use. Indeed, many of our learners are already using tools like instant messaging in their personal lives.

d The need for either text or voice chat conventions will depend on the size of the group in the chat. Usually if a chat is held between only two participants conventions are unnecessary, but for larger groups conventions are a good idea, especially for text chat.

e Conducting initial chat practice sessions with a class who already know each other is a good idea, but our feeling is that chat should then be used in a 'real' situation, with learners using chat to contact learners who are not in the same place. For the use of chat to be meaningful for learners, and not just a gimmick in class, we would suggest that chat is used outside class between class members or between two classes who are in geographically separate places.

B

1 Either **2** Either **3** Voice **4** Voice **5** Text **6** Either

C

1 a 4 **b** 2 **c** 1 **d** 3

2 1 task-oriented **2** informative or collaborative (depending on how the chat is run, and whether learners then need to do something with the information they learn) **3** practice **4** informative or collaborative (depending on how the chat is run, and whether learners then need to do something with the information they learn) **5** practice **6** free topic

Chapter 7

A

1 d **2** l **3** f **4** a **5** m **6** g **7** e **8** b **9** n **10** c **11** j **12** i **13** k **14** h

B

1 S **2** T **3** T **4** C **5** C or S **6** C

C

1 A blog is essentially an online journal or diary, usually written by one person, which is added to regularly. Most blogs allow visitors to add comments, which are then visible to the blog owner, and also to subsequent visitors who can in turn comment further. A wiki, on the other hand, is like a public website, or public web page, started by one person, but which subsequent visitors can add to, delete or change as they wish. Instead of being a static web page or website like a blog, a wiki is more dynamic, and can have multiple authors. A wiki is like having a publicly accessible word processed document available online, which anyone can edit.

2 Activities 1, 5, 6.

D

	Advantages	Disadvantages
Learners listen to podcasts	• low-level EFL/ESL podcasts available for low-level learners. • high levels can be exposed to authentic podcasts. • podcasts good for self-study (learners can listen to them where and when they want). • teacher introduces a new medium into the classroom. • podcast content can be stimulating and up-to-date.	• learners need an MP3 player or similar.

Learners create podcasts	• learners use a new ICT tool, and create their own content (motivating). • learners can in theory reach a world-wide audience. • learners will take extra care in preparation and presentation knowing that there is a wider audience. • podcasts can look and sound very professional.	• teacher needs a microphone connected to the computer to record the podcast. • learners may feel overly pressured to 'get it right'.

Chapter 8
A
Good reasons: 1, 2, 4, 7

Potential disadvantages: 3, 5 (if considered as exclusive, and not catering for other learner styles), 6
B
1 translator **2** thesaurus **3** dictionary **4** concordancer **5** encyclopedia

Chapter 9
A
1 listening **2** writing **3** authentic **4** multiple choice **5** reorder sentences **6** Free writing
7 speaking
B

Courseware	Advantage	Disadvantage
CD-ROMs	Encourages autonomous learning.	Voice recognition software can be unreliable.
Computer-based testing	Reliability in marking is high.	Speaking and writing are difficult to assess reliably.
Interactive whiteboards	Materials in this medium look very impressive.	Costs are high for the average teacher/school.

Chapter 10
A
a 5 **b** 4 **c** 6 **d** 2 **e** 1 **f** 3
B
1 **c** Create a new maze.

2 **f** Give your reading maze a title.

3 **b** Add a title to Decision Point 1.

4 **i** Describe the basic situation in Decision Point 1, giving two options to choose from.

5 **e** Create a link to a new Decision Point (Decision Point 2).

6 **j** Create a link to a new Decision Point (Decision Point 3).

7 **a** Change to view Decision Point 2, and write the content.

8 **g** Change to view Decision Point 3, and write the content.

9 d Save your maze.

10 h Export your reading maze to XHTML (make it into a web page).

Chapter 11
A
Commentary:

3, 4. Although all of the above are examples of 'e-learning', as they include the use of electronic media, only 3 and 4 are online learning, as they involve a major part of course delivery and course work taking place virtually over the Internet.

B

Advantages	Disadvantages
• Study at own pace, in own time. • Travel costs reduced and time saved. • Have access to courses they might otherwise be unable to attend. • For asynchronous communication, have time to prepare responses, so accuracy may be better. • Content can be kept very up-to-date. • The Internet can provide a wealth of additional material/resources. • Tutor feedback can be highly individualised.	• May feel isolated. • Unrealistic expectations. • Some skills are more difficult to practise online (e.g. speaking). • A high degree of self-motivation is usually needed. • Technical issues and access may cause problems. • Drop-out rates tend to be slightly higher online than face-to-face.

C

I recently joined the group – voluntary membership

using ICT tools with your students – a negotiated goal

led by Danny G – a core member

a class blog at www.classblog.blogspot.com – an artefact

I realise now I should have asked you all if you could come and post to our blog before we started – reflection on practice

Chapter 12
A
a image repository **b** music management **c** shared desktops **d** media bank **e** large file transfers **f** shared wisdom **g** life goals collection **h** online calendar **i** news portal **j** project management
B
a a Content Management System **b** Second Life **c** MP3 players **d** mobile phones **e** a Virtual Learning Environment

GLOSSARY

Explanation

This glossary contains entries for all the technology terms cited in bold in *How to Teach English with Technology*. In the following entry the main heading (Ask.com) is in **bold**. Because 'search engine' is written in SMALL CAPITALS, this means that there is an entry for that in the glossary too. The symbol → means that you should (also) look at that entry.

Ask.com – a well-known search engine, which allows real language searches. → SEARCH ENGINE

asynchronous (adj.)– not happening in real time. Asynchronous communication is not immediate, such as communication by email. → SYNCHRONOUS

Audacity – audio blogging software.

Audioblog – audio blogging software.

authoring tool – a program that allows the user to produce multimedia content in the form of web pages.

avatar – a 3-dimensional cartoon-like representation of oneself, used in virtual worlds such as Second Life.

beamer → DATA PROJECTOR

blended learning – learning which involves a combination of e-learning and face-to-face learning.

blog – an abbreviation of the term 'weblog'. A blog is a regularly updated journal or newsletter in the form of a web page, usually kept by one individual, and intended for public consumption.

blogroll – a list of links to blogs.

browse – to visit web pages on the Internet.

CALL (**Computer Assisted Language Learning**) – an approach to language teaching and learning which uses computer technology.

CD-ROM – a circular disk which looks like a music CD, but can store a range of data such as text, videos, audio files or images.

chat – real-time communication over the Internet.

chatware – software for voice and/or text chat. Chat programs you may come across are: Qnext, .NET Messenger Service, Jabber, QQ, iChat and ICQ. → INSTANT MESSAGING

class blog – a blog in which a group of students participate.

commenting privileges – the right of access to invited members of a blog.

community of practice (**CoP**)– a group that shares experience and knowledge.

computer room – a classroom with a number of computers which can be connected to each other and/or the Internet.

concordancer – a computer program that counts and lists the occurrences of a given term, showing examples of its use from a corpus (or body) of text. → CORPUS and WORDSMITH TOOLS

Content Management System (**CMS**) – a web-based software system allowing for the management of large quantities of content (documents, multimedia, etc) and the collaborative creation of documents.

corpus (s.); **corpuses, corpora** (pl.) – a corpus is an amount of collected texts, held in a computer, which can be accessed and analysed by means of a concordancer. Corpuses can be based on spoken text, or on written text. Well-known corpuses are the British National Corpus, and the COBUILD Bank of English corpus. → CONCORDANCER and WORDSMITH TOOLS

coursecasting – a situation where a teacher delivers course content to students as downloads.

database – a collection of information stored on a computer or a CD-ROM in a systematic way, so that it can be easily accessed.

data projector – also known as an LCD (Liquid Crystal Display) projector, or a 'beamer', a data projector is connected to a computer, and projects what is seen on the computer onto a large screen. Often used for PowerPoint presentations.

digital divide – the gap between those with access to technology and those without.

digital immigrant – an individual who has come late to the world of technology.

digital native – an individual who is comfortable and confident with new technology.

discussion group – an electronic list in which list members correspond by email to discuss issues of interest to the group. A discussion group will typically not only receive and send emails, but will also have access to a group website where they can save and share files, use chat, and read other members' profiles. → MAILING LIST

discussion list – a mailing list that enables and encourages discussion.

DVD – an abbreviation for 'Digital Versatile Disc'. A circular disc which looks like a CD-ROM, but can store more data.

edublog – a blog with an educational purpose.

e-learning – an abbreviation for 'electronic learning', and refers to learning which involves the use of electronic media, such as the Internet, CD-ROMs, DVDs, or mobile devices such as MP3 players and PDAs (Personal Digital Assistants). e-learning can be face-to-face or distance.

email – an abbreviation of the term 'electronic mail'. Written messages which are transmitted from one user to another via the Internet. The messages may include attached files. There are several free email services available on the Internet, such as Hotmail and Google Mail (or 'Gmail').

emoticons – symbols used in written electronic communication (such as emails, instant messaging and texting) to denote emotions. For example pleasure can be denoted by a smiley face using these symbols : -). Note that emoticons need to be 'read' (looked at) sideways.

ePortfolio – a digital collection of an individual student's work and achievements.

floppy disk – a thin, flexible plastic disk which stores computer data. As floppy disks have limited storage capacity (typically around 1.4MB), they are being increasingly replaced by CDs, DVDs and USB pen drives, which can usually store much larger amounts.

Freevlog – video blogging software.

Google – a well-known search engine, which allows keyword searches. → SEARCH ENGINE

Google Mail – a free email service, provided by Google. Also known as 'Gmail'. → EMAIL

Hotmail – a free email service, provided by Microsoft. → EMAIL

ICT (**Information and Communications Technology**) – technology used for processing, storing and retrieving information, as well as for communication.

instant messaging – a form of electronic communication via text chat, in which users are online simultaneously, and communication takes place in real time. Many instant messaging programs also include voice chat, and one-to-one video-conferencing via web cameras. Well-known instant messaging programs are: Yahoo! Messenger, MSN Messenger, Google Talk, Skype, and AOL Instant Messenger.

interactive whiteboard (**IWB**) – an electronically enhanced whiteboard, used in face-to-face teaching, which allows content from a computer screen to be projected onto the whiteboard. Images and text can be manipulated by using a special electronic pen.

Internet – a global network of computers, which allow users to access websites, communicate and exchange information. Also known as 'the web' or 'the net'. → WEB

Internet café – a place where one can go to access the Internet.

Internet surfer – an individual who spends a lot of time looking for and at content on the Internet.

IT (**Information Technology**) – the study or use of technology for processing, storing and retrieving information.

keypal – the electronic equivalent of a pen pal. Keypals are friends who communicate using electronic media – they exchange emails instead of traditional paper-based letters. → PEN PAL

keyword – a significant (or 'key') word or phrase, that can be used in a search engine to find information about a specific topic.

kinaesthetic learners – learners who learn best through activities involving movement, or by 'doing' things.

LCD projector → DATA PROJECTOR

Learner Management System (**LMS**) – a learning platform within which students can work together on line.

mailing list – an electronic list in which list members exchange information by email. → DISCUSSION GROUP

memory stick → USB PEN DRIVE

meta search – a search which uses multiple search engines, and combines the results into a single page. A well-known meta search engine is Meta Search (http://www.metasearch.com).

Microsoft Excel – a popular spreadsheet program produced by Microsoft in which data can be inserted and manipulated. It is part of Microsoft Office.

Microsoft NetMeeting – video-conferencing software developed by Microsoft and included in many Microsoft Windows packages.
→ Windows Meeting Space

Microsoft Office – a popular suite of programs produced by Microsoft which includes Word, Excel, Office and PowerPoint.

Microsoft PowerPoint – a popular presentation package produced by Microsoft in which digital slides can be produced and manipulated on the computer, then projected onto a screen using a data projector. It is part of Microsoft Office.

Microsoft Word – a popular word processing program produced by Microsoft in which texts can be produced and manipulated. It is part of Microsoft Office.

mixed technological ability – a situation where a group of students have varying levels of computer skills.

m-learning – learning which involves the use of mobile electronic media, such as MP3 players, PDAs (Personal Digital Assistants) or mobile phones.

MP3 player – a small portable device used for listening to audio files in a compressed format called MP3. You can download audio MP3 files from the Internet onto your computer, or from a CD, and then transfer these files to an MP3 player to listen to later.

MUVE – Multi-User Virtual Environment.

netiquette – the 'rules' or guidelines that govern polite behaviour and interaction online.

Netizen – an individual who uses the Internet in a social way.

offline – not connected to the Internet. One can write an email offline, for example, then go online (connect to the Internet) to send it.

online – connected to the Internet.

OpenOffice – an open source office suite, similar to Microsoft Office.

open source – software which is usually freely available on the Internet, and to which anyone with the necessary programming skills can contribute. Well-known open source software includes the operating system Linux, and the VLE Moodle.

pbwiki – software for the creation of wikis.

PDA (**Personal Digital Assistant**) – also known as palmtops, handheld computers or pocket computers, PDAs are handheld devices that combine computing, telephone/fax, and networking features. A typical PDA can function as a mobile phone, fax sender, and personal diary. Many PDAs incorporate handwriting and/or voice recognition features.

peer-to-peer (**P2P**) – a technology that allows for informal networks of computers to share resources. In P2P networking, downloads are split into much smaller chunks of data and sent via the network of connected computers, enabling quicker file transfers.

pen pal – pen pals are friends who communicate using traditional paper-based letters. → keypal

podcast – a method of publishing usually audio files on the Internet. A user can subscribe to these files (often at no cost), and download them to his/her computer and to a portable listening device such as an MP3 player.

PodClip – a video podcast.

podOmatic – podcast creation software.

portal – a website that provides access to a number of resources and services, including links to other websites, a facility to search for other sites, news, e-mail, phone and map information, and sometimes a community forum.

role-play (v.)– to take on a character, to play a part. In language learning this is used to practice language in contexts similar to real life.

role-play (n.)– the activity of taking on a character.

RSS (**Really Simple Syndication**) – software which organises online sources of information for the individual.

screenshot – a printed or captured image taken from a computer program.

search engine – a tool or program which helps users find information on the Internet. Two well-known search engines are Yahoo! and Google.

Second Life – a new Internet environment which has a virtual reality.

self-access centre (**SAC**) – a classroom which can be used by learners to study alone. A SAC often has computers, and access to the Internet, as well as CD-ROMs, books, magazines, etc.

self-study – a mode of learning in which learners work alone, often without the aid of a teacher, either at home or in a self-access centre.

server – a computer system that operates a network.

Skype – a software program which uses peer-to-peer data transfer techniques to facilitate free audio and video conversations over the Internet. This is often referred to as VoIP (Voice over Internet Protocol) technology.

social bookmarking – allowing other people to view an individual's bookmarks.

social software – software that creates links between individuals.

spam – unsolicited information sent by email, spam often tries to sell you something. Computer users often install anti-spam software, or use a spam filter with their email program to try to avoid receiving too much spam.

storage capacity – the amount of space available for content in digital form.

student blog – a blog which an individual student sets up and maintains.

subject guide – the way in which a search engine divides its content into subject areas.

synchronous (adj.) – happening in real time. Synchronous communication is immediate, such as communication by instant messenger, or by telephone. → ASYNCHRONOUS

technogeek – an individual who is enthusiastic about new technology.

technophobe – an individual who is not comfortable and confident with new technology.

TELL (**Technology Enhanced Language Learning**) – derived from the term CALL, this is an approach to language teaching and learning which uses a range of technology and electronic media.

texting – a form of communication whereby text messages are sent between users via mobile phones.

text wrapping – a way of formatting text in a document so that the text flows around an inserted graphic.

tracking facility – the ability to monitor student performance.

tutor blog – a blog led by a teacher.

url – an abbreviation of the term 'uniform resource locator', meaning website address. An example is http://www.wikipedia.org. → WEBSITE

USB pen drive – also known as a 'memory stick', this is a small device which can store large amounts of data. Useful for carrying files and information from one computer to another.

video conferencing – a meeting between people who are not physically present, via computers connected to the Internet, using technologies such as video cameras and audio tools, simultaneously.

Virtual Learning Environments (**VLEs**) – a software system designed to help teachers manage online educational courses. VLEs generally include course content, communication tools, grading tools, student tracking, grouping facilities and control over who accesses the course. VLEs are also known as 'platforms', Managed Learning Environments (MLEs), and Learner Management Systems (LMSs).

virus – a program or piece of code that is often carried by email. Once a virus inserts itself into your computer, it can cause serious damage, although some viruses are harmless. Computer users often install anti-virus software to protect themselves against computer viruses.

Vodcast – a video podcast.

voice recognition software – software used for pronunciation practice which analyses performance.

vlog – short for video blog.

web – a global network of computers, which allow users to access websites, communicate and exchange information. → INTERNET

web browser – software that allows a computer user to see and interact with content on a website.

webcam – an abbreviation of 'web camera'. A small camera which is connected to a computer, and can record video or take photos. Instant messaging programs usually allow users to see each other with webcams, and to simultaneously communicate via voice and text chat.

webquest – a project which requires learners to use Internet resources and websites to find information. A webquest has four main stages: Introduction, Task, Process and Evaluation.

website – a collection of files on the Internet, which can be accessed by a user via a single 'url' or website address.

wiki – a series of collaborative web pages to which anyone can contribute. Changes to the wiki web pages are automatically saved, and can be retrieved and restored. Many wikis are password protected – in this case, only users with the password can make changes to the wiki content.

Wikipedia – an online encyclopedia.

Windows Meeting Space – video-conferencing software developed by Microsoft, and included in the Microsoft Windows Vista package. At the time of print, it is set to replace Microsoft NetMeeting. → MICROSOFT NETMEETING

word processing program – a program which allows you to write, edit and design your text on screen.

WordSmith Tools – a concordancer produced by Oxford University Press. → CORPUS and CONCORDANCER

Yahoo! – a well-known search engine, which allows subject searches. → SEARCH ENGINE

Yahoo! Groups – free software available for discussion groups. Features of Yahoo! Groups include chat, file storage facilities, a list of group members and profiles, a poll facility, a calendar, a photo album and user statistics (such as the number of postings in a month).

INDEX

Note: References in *italic* are to the Task File and Key.

CD-ROM instructions

Starting and installing the CD-ROM
If you are using Windows
Insert CD in drive and it will start automatically.
You can choose:
1 Run from CD
2 Install – you may need administrator privileges
If you are using Mac OS 9
Double-click on the file called HTTEWT_OS9 to run the program. To install, copy all of the files to your hard disk.
If you are using Mac OS X
Double-click on the file called HTTEWT_MacOSX to run the program. To install, copy all of the files to your hard disk.
If you are using the Linux operating system
Mount CD and then click on the file called HTTEWT_Linux. To install, copy all of the files to your hard disk.

What's on the CD-ROM?
For each of the twelve chapters you can hear real teachers from around the world talking about their experience of using new technology in their teaching. If you want to, you can read the audioscripts while you listen to what they have to say, and print the audioscripts out for later reference.

In addition to these recordings, there are nine video tutorials you can watch:
Using TrackChanges (Chapter 2)
Webquest creation (Chapter 4) [+ screenshot of C12 contents]
A keypal project (Chapter 5)
Setting up a Skype account (Chapter 6)
How to set up your own account in Blogger (Chapter 7)
Using Hot Potatoes (Chapter 10)
Joining Webheads (Chapter 11)
Using RSS (Really Simple Syndication) (Chapter 12)
Second Life (Chapter 12).

You can also go on a tour of a Longman dictionary (Chapter 8) and see a short video of an interactive whiteboard in action in a real classroom (Chapter 9). Lastly, there is an interactive Webliography for each chapter for further research.

System specification (minimum)

Windows	Macintosh	Linux
98/NT/2000/ME/XP	PowerPC processor 300Mhz	Redhat, Mandrake 9.2,
Pentium 350Mhz	OS 9.2.2 & OSX	GNU/Linux, GNU Debian.
64 MB RAM	96MB RAM	64MB RAM

Note: When you come to view and use the applications demonstrated in the nine tutorials, you may find that there are minor differences in the way the software works. This is because the programs are being continually updated.

For support please contact ELT-Support@pearson.com